The Myriad
Gifts *of*
ASPERGER'S
SYNDROME

of related interest

The Complete Guide to Asperger's Syndrome
Tony Attwood
ISBN 978 1 84310 495 7

Natural Genius
The Gift of Asperger's Syndrome
Susan Rubinyi
ISBN 978 1 84310 784 2

The Genesis of Artistic Creativity
Asperger's Syndrome and the Arts
Michael Fitzgerald
ISBN 978 1 84310 334 9

Asperger's Syndrome and High Achievement
Some Very Remarkable People
Ioan James
ISBN 978 1 84310 388 2

Bright Splinters of the Mind
A Personal Story of Research with Autistic Savants
Beate Hermelin
Foreword by Sir Michael Rutter
ISBN 978 1 85302 932 5

An Exact Mind
An Artist With Asperger Syndrome
Peter Myers, Simon Baron-Cohen and Sally Wheelwright
ISBN 978 1 84310 032 4

Asperger Syndrome and Employment
A Personal Guide to Succeeding at Work
Nick Dubin, with Gail Hawkins
DVD ISBN 978 1 84310 849 8

Realizing the College Dream with Autism or Asperger Syndrome
A Parent's Guide to Student Success
Ann Palmer
ISBN 978 1 84310 801 6

A Self-Determined Future with Asperger Syndrome
Solution Focused Approaches
E. Veronica Bliss and Genevieve Edmonds
ISBN 978 1 84310 513 8

The Myriad
Gifts *of*
ASPERGER'S
SYNDROME

JOHN M. ORTIZ Ph. D.

Jessica Kingsley Publishers
London and Philadelphia

This edition published in 2008
by Jessica Kingsley Publishers
116 Pentonville Road
London N1 9JB, UK
and
400 Market Street, Suite 400
Philadelphia, PA 19106, USA
www.jkp.com

First published in the United States in 2005 as The Gifts of Asperger's syndrome by
The Asperger's Syndrome Institute

Library of Congress Cataloging in Publication Data
Ortiz, John M.
    The gifts of Asperger's syndrome / John M. Ortiz.
        p. cm.
    Includes bibliographical references.
    ISBN 978-1-84310-883-2 (pb : alk. paper) 1. Asperger's syndrome. 2. Asperger's
syndrome--Patients--Case studies. I. Title.
    RC553.A88O78 2008
    616.85'8832--dc22

2007030641

British Library Cataloguing in Publication Data
A CIP catalogue record for this book is available from the British Library

ISBN 978 1 84310 883 2

Printed and bound in the United States by
Thomson-Shore, 7300 Joy Road, Dexter, MI, 48130

This book is dedicated to Michael
without whose inspiration this dedication
would have no occasion.

Contents

The Asperger Dimension

Imagine living in an alternative dimension where everyone follows traffic rules; salespeople are honest; telemarketers only call based on personal requests; news is based on actual facts; politicians follow through on their stated promises; no contracts have "small print" (this is no longer needed, since every detail is fully spelled out in plain, clear language); airline flights are never overbooked; warranties specify unambiguous facts and are consistently upheld along with their product's patent guarantees; businesses follow through on their promises and responsibilities; repair persons arrive at your home on time as scheduled; people say exactly what they think/feel without playing mind games (there is no longer any need for "fuzzy interpretations" or "mind reading"); and people do not talk behind each other's backs, but, rather, say what they feel directly to your face, good, bad, or neutral. In relationships, partners do not lie, cheat, or allow issues to drag on; they do not use control tactics, subtle manipulations, deception, or "silent treatments," but, instead, when partnerships begin to disintegrate, they present you with direct statements such as: "I think we no longer have a lot in common and should go our separate ways."

This would be a dimension where people pursue careers and take on jobs that are based on their skills and passions, rather than how much money a particular trade may earn them or what status it may provide, and thus they become ultimate specialists in their vocational pursuits. Workers do not call in sick unless their ill health warrants it, and do not cheat or lie to gain unfair advantages, sabotage their coworkers, or even as much as take another person's parking spot.

Asher is genuine. As with other Asperger's people, what you see is what you get. He seems incapable of duplicity. So refreshing. When I hear corruption stories on the news I often think…what if the executives at Enron had a touch of Asperger's? The judge could ask them, straight up: "Hey guys—what is it with all those Shell companies?" Asperger's executives would spew forth a fountain of answers in painstaking detail. Case closed. (Coursey 2005, p.308)

Courses taken in college, and majors pursued, reflect areas of true academic interest, aimed at what students *want* to do with their lives, rather than what they think they *should* do, or what career paths may appear to them to be the most lucrative regardless of their professional and personal interests. In this dimension, rather than people looking at you and not listening, they would be actively listening and processing—and would ask you to slow down, repeat, or clarify comments they may not fully understand—rather than looking at you but not focusing on, hearing, or understanding what you are actually saying. If, during the conversation, you lost your train of thought, the listener's superior focus and memory skills would help you to refresh or repeat what you were saying. If the person you were speaking to was not interested in you or your topic, they would simply tell you so, rather than pretending they care or talk about how uninteresting you are soon after your back is turned.

In this alternative dimension, whenever you check into a hotel, the site honors your reservation, and the room that you requested and reserved weeks or months in advance is waiting for you upon your arrival, along with the amenities that were included with your request or package. Upon checkout, you can be assured that no hidden charges will appear on your bill.

In this wonderful dimension people do not have hidden agendas. Here, educators and mental health practitioners are paid in actual proportion to their societal worth, and valued in status in relation to their potential benefit to society. This would also be a dimension where criminals own up to their crimes rather than externalizing blame or lying about their misdeeds. They admit to their crimes even though they realize it was "wrong," and they understand that their transgressions cannot be "undone," or the harm they have caused others repaired. Through criminals' admissions of guilt, the victims and/or their families and loved ones will at least know that the person who committed the offense can be rightfully punished, that debts to society will be paid, and money otherwise wasted in prosecution will be saved. This potential dimension will see people treated according to their behaviors and characteristics, rather than the color of their skin, religious preference, ethnicity, political orientation, neurological differences, family background and status, and so on. In effect, all men and women will be paid and treated equally, according to standard guidelines without fear of discrimination, favoritism, or prejudice. Here, an individual's personal characteristics will have no bearing on hiring, firing, promotions, salaries, or anything that do not impinge on their actual vocational talents, abilities, or work-related behaviors.

In this nearly magical dimension, the food we consume and the environment we live in would not be littered or contaminated with toxic chemicals and refuse because the highly sensitive people inhabiting it would be well aware of the harms of toxicity. Additionally, being dedicated specialists in their fields and savvy consumers, they would take responsibility for ensuring the quality of ecologically healthy and environmentally friendly products. The well-focused researchers and dedicated scientists would apply their natural perseverance and tireless determination to ensure that the systems they design, and products they use, would be safe for consumers, many of whom were their own friends and families. A new level of quality control, then, would be customarily applied that would provide the highest possible standards to ensure uncontaminated, harmless, toxin-free foods, products, and environments without unsafe additives, injurious chemicals, or risky preservatives. Homes, schools, businesses, department stores, and other places of public access would have no fluorescent lights, or detrimental noises, scents, lethal insulation systems, noxious gases, and hazardous levels of radiation or contamination.

The above is not a magical, imaginary world. It is simply the Asperger dimension.

> I like to imagine every bigwig involved with Social Security with Asperger's. We could all rest assured that the matter would be resolved with utmost transparency. I also like to imagine filling the entire Capitol building and White House with Asperger's people, along with every boardroom and executive suite. Lots of people with Asperger's have no internal dialogue; they offer a running commentary on their thoughts, impressions, and intentions. We would always have a ready report on exactly what's going on. (Coursey 2005, p.309)

CHAPTER 1

*I*ntroduction

Background

On October 1, 1961, at the age of nine, I boarded an airplane for the first time in my life. The plane was to be my magic carpet taking me from my homeland, in Havana, Cuba, and the tyrannical clutches of the Castro government, to the safety and freedom of the United States. After a short flight, I arrived at Miami airport. After a little more than nine hours of anxiously sitting at the airport watching thousands of strangers come and go, my mother's relatives, who had sponsored my entry into the United States, finally arrived for me.

During those seemingly endless nine hours the thoughts of never seeing either of my parents, my baby sister, or anyone I had ever known again, played like an endless, tragic loop in my mind. I spoke not a word of English. I was lonely, hungry and very, very scared. Eventually, I met my relatives for the first time and was introduced to life in the United States.

A few weeks later, my parents and four-year-old sister were given permission to leave the country and, gradually, they joined me in the United States. Within a relatively short time, we received enough support from extended family members to enable us to settle into a place of our own in south Miami. United once again, after months of sitting idle, it was finally time for me to enroll in an American school, a fantasy that I had long dreamed about.

In early November I was taken to the local school for enrollment. After a couple of hours of red tape, I was escorted to an office where I was given a battery of tests. Because the tests were in English, a language I did not speak—an obvious handicap that was inexplicably ignored by the school's evaluator—I did not do well. In fact, I did so poorly that the results that came a few days later indicated a painful finding. The diagnostic impression was that I was "mentally retarded." This was quite a perplexing conclusion judging from the fact that, just a few weeks earlier, I had been attending a highly selective, private, European school back in Cuba, excelling in curricula that would have been the equivalent of what we today know as "gifted classes."

Back in the early 1960s, of course, there were no special classes for the "intellectually challenged." There was no special ed, no alternative classrooms, no remedial courses, no tutors. Instead, that niche was filled by what was referred to as—I would learn sometime later—"holding tanks for the undesirables." The "undesirables" was an all-inclusive term that encompassed children currently described as oppositional, conduct disordered, bullies, and other "difficult children" who presented problems for the school, as well as those with any number of mental, emotional and physical challenges.

As my father's quest for available jobs necessitated various moves throughout South Florida over the next 21 months, "the label" that had been stamped in my records, but much more injuriously burrowing deep within my self-esteem, was not easily shaken. Because children may not be as fragile as glass bottles, but, unlike bottles, once labels are placed on them it is impossible to ever completely remove them.

> A label, depending on one's viewpoint, can be one of the most stigmatizing things a majority can inflict on an individual. It's the power of the majority asserted over the minority. A label, psychiatric or otherwise, is a convenient short-hand symbol for defining you as a person... I don't want to have AS define me as a human being, partly because I don't think any finite cluster of words and ideas ever could. ("Peter," quoted in Stoddart 2005, p.313)

During that time, regardless of the school or district where my parents would relocate, I was confused with the "undesirables." Instructional techniques in those "special classes" ranged from absolute indifference from the hapless teacher who happened to be stuck babysitting the "inmates" for the hour, to blatant sadistic treatment from teachers who thrived on intimidation—verbal, emotional and physical abuse.

Eventually, after fighting an uphill, exasperating and demeaning 18-month battle with the South Florida school systems, prejudice, and lack of working opportunities, my parents decided that we needed to move away. The second airplane ride of my life occurred at that time. This time, the flight would take me far, far away to a magical land where children were mainstreamed and were not given unfair, lifelong, damaging and inescapable labels. In this new land I would be allowed to mix with "the regular kids," be placed in "regular classes," and "take regular courses." Those two years in hell, however, would be lost forever, and the scars, seemingly, will never go away.

A few years later, having had the opportunity to master the English language, I was again given an IQ battery. This time my full-scale score was found to be 129. Two later tests in subsequent years yielded scores of 136 and 148.

Fast forward to the early 1990s. As the end of the twentieth century approached, the trend of "political correctness" bringing a mixed aware-ness to cultural, ethnic, racial and other forms of diversity seemed to be at an all time high. Minority groups all over the country were gaining more recognition and "tolerance" became a very popular word. During those 30-odd years between my arrival in the United States and unfolding of "tolerance," testing and evaluation in schools grew by quantum leaps. Alternative classrooms, special education, inclusion, mainstreaming, "leave no child behind," and many other avenues of opportunity were now avail-able for those who were "different," "challenged," "unique," or whatever other words seemed to sound the least harmful and most empowering for the children. And this was certainly a step in the right direction.

Although the advances throughout our educational, mental health, social service, therapeutic, medical and other systems of the early 1990s had grown tremendously, a new wave of diversity was just about to strike the United States, and the world, in unprecedented ways. That wave, which arrived somewhat like a tsunami, was officially declared in 1994 with the American Psychiatric Association's publication of the fourth version of the *Diagnostic Statistical Manual*. Unfolding a tapestry of neurodiversity, the crest of the wave was called Asperger's Disorder, or, as it is more correctly referred to, "Asperger's Syndrome."

Classified under the spectrum of "Pervasive Developmental," or "Autistic" disorders, Asperger's Syndrome (AS) in many ways served to extend the autistic spectrum into the "challenged but good" area. Suddenly, the old notion of autism being a severely troubling and limiting disorder took on a new light. Children with autism, we found, would not automatically grow up to be schizophrenic adults or be restricted to institutions and sheltered workshops. In fact, persons with autism who fell under the Asperger's umbrella often grew up to be fully functioning adults excelling in fields like computer science, mathematics, physics, engineering, accounting and others that stretched throughout the fabric of society. To many parents, then, AS brought hope, promise and a universe of possibilities for their children that could be realized through early detection, nurturing, support, patience and understanding. AS became a "good" autism.

> What I admire most about my boys, especially Zack, is the courage, strength, and character that they have to keep going back out every day into what can often seem like a war zone; coming home, worn, tired, and stressed at having tried to keep it together for the day, and getting up the next day to do it again... My sons' uniqueness and way of looking at things has altered my way of seeing the world. I look at this as their gift to me. ("Margot," quoted in Stoddart 2005, p.350)

The Discovery of Michael

On April 1, 1992, my nephew Michael was born in South Florida. A happy, physically beautiful, highly intelligent child who could read by the age of two, charm the uncharmable, and bring a smile to anyone's soul. By the age of three, Michael was a fairly fluent reader who could memorize and recite entire passages from books, dialogues from videos and countless songs with which he would entertain anyone and everyone who would listen. Context was inconsequential, and shyness never an issue. The information that he had compiled by the age of four was staggering. His language was on par with children three times his age, and his fund of knowledge increased by the day. It seemed that anything he learned, he would not forget. By this point, he was even correcting poor grammar, spelling and mispronounced words. Michael was different. So much so that no one who met him knew what to make of him. Gifted? Surely. Unusual? Certainly. Shortly afterward, Michael was given a battery of tests. Although he could certainly speak English, he did not do well. In fact, he did so poorly that the results that came in a few days later indicated that he was, inexplicably, "mentally retarded."

Fortunately, Michael was surrounded by an enviable, unwavering family support system that would come to his aid like Alexander the Great's famed cavalry. More importantly, perhaps, was the fact that two members of his family just happened to be licensed, doctoral-level psychologists. Shortly after his "diagnosis" was made, the family resources clicked into high gear, and no stone was left unturned in the efforts to find a realistic, and accurate, "label" for the magical child. After a few months of searching, investigating, reading, and consulting with professionals of every modality, that label was "Asperger's Syndrome with hyperlexia."

(Note: Hyperlexia is a syndrome that is characterized by a precocious phonetic decoding, or "reading," ability that far exceeds expectations at an early chronological age—at times as prematurely as 18–24 months—but usually without actual comprehension of what is being read. It often also involves a fascination with numbers or letters and can include difficulties with pragmatic speech, nonverbal learning difficulties, and problems with reciprocal interaction.)

Fast forward to 2005. Thirteen-year-old Michael is now an eighth-grader enrolled in gifted classes in Georgia. "Autistic children *are* able to produce original ideas. Indeed, they can *only* be original" (Asperger 1991, p.70).

The "discovery of Michael" has had stunning effects on the many lives that he has touched. His effect on me, for one, has been incalculable. Although I was already a practicing psychologist when he was born, specializing on helping children and adolescents with special challenges and unique talents, I still felt unfulfilled in my career. Regardless of how hard I worked, the impacts I made, and the differences I was making in people's lives, I still felt that I was falling far short from realizing my potential, or even finding my professional niche. The "discovery of Michael," however, changed all of that, effectively reshaping my career and life's path.

When Michael came into the picture, his situation seemed to somehow bookend my own. Both of us had been grossly misjudged and mislabeled by an obsolete system that failed us miserably. It was our good fortune that, due to our nurturing and supremely supportive immediate and extended families, we were both given the opportunity to prove ourselves and share our talents, intellect, and creativity with the world.

Many other children, however, are not so fortunate. Whether because of exhausted single parents, poorly trained or overworked educators, or myriad other reasons, countless children fall prey to circumstances from which they cannot escape. Sometimes, a special teacher comes to the rescue. Other times, it may be a relative. Other times, it may be someone completely unexpected, who steps in at just the right time and place, and triggers a thought, gives advice, or introduces us to a path or notion that had, to that point, been blocked or laid hidden. I was fortunate enough to have several special teachers, relatives, and unexpected people in my life. Because of those fortunate events at random times throughout my developmental stages, I am writing these words today with the hope that those who read them may be able to better recognize the glistening gifts that often lie hidden, just beneath the troubled surface.

Having bookended my life, "the discovery of Michael" gave me the energy, ambition, and direction that I had so sorely been lacking in my professional life. As other family members sacrificed their lives to assure that Michael would receive the best of all possible care—socially, academically, emotionally, and spiritually—I longed to do my part. At first, it was to learn as much as I possibly could about this mysterious condition. The more I learned about it, I felt, the better we could join together in our collective understanding of Michael and his unique situation. He has so many strengths, yet many of them seemed somehow hidden, just out of reach. These are the gifts of Asperger's Syndrome being blocked by the puzzles of autism.

During my early, relentless quest to learn all I could about Asperger's in particular, and autism spectrum disorders in general, I began to realize that there was very, very little known about it at the time. Finding relevant, helpful, and practical information during those early years was frustratingly difficult. Since a popular notion among many at that time was that AS was either "a very rare condition" that afflicted a diminutive (and, as such, "inconsequential") segment of the population, or perhaps even something that "doesn't even exist," many avenues where I would ordinarily turn to for help where unavailable, uninterested, or uninformed. Obtaining accurate information presented a new challenge in my life. Through diligence, persistence, and "looking beyond the box," however, the rewards that have come with unearthing the gifts of this fascinating condition have been an explorer's dream come true.

The Box

Beware the child who sets aside the toy and plays with the box. Almost everything that we deal with in our daily lives involves some sort of box or form of enclosure. When we buy a computer, for instance, it comes in a box. Once we open the main box, we find, neatly packed inside, an array of smaller boxes, all fitting perfectly snug against each other like a finely engineered puzzle. If, during the course of using the computer, we find that something is amiss, or we are dissatisfied with our purchase and choose to return it, the product and all of its components need to be returned in their original box. Inside the large box, we must somehow then figure out how to fit all of the sundry little boxes carefully designed to occupy every single nook and cranny when packed at the factory.

Business cards, iPods, file folders, picture frames, stereo components, speakers, television sets, psychological tests, cigars, coffee makers, hair curlers…just about everything we purchase comes in its own tidy, little box. Many of us, in fact, come up with myriad creative ways of using some of these boxes for secondary purposes. As a child, I fondly recall waiting patiently for a local appliance store to discard their refrigerator boxes, which we would convert into clubhouses. Large TV boxes became towers, or "additions" to these childhood domiciles. Shoe boxes, it seems, are almost universally intended for family photographs and tax receipts. Hat boxes, on the other hand, are often reserved for the more precious, sentimental mementos. I also clearly recall my sisters and I furiously fighting over our grandfather's freshly discarded cigar boxes as if they were priceless artifacts. In effect, sometimes the life of these boxes tends to long outlast that of the object they originally protected. Shoe and hat boxes filled with family treasures, for instance, often fill their space within our closets (another box) long after the shoes they contained have worn out and the hats have been donated or discarded after going out of style.

Although the name for these enclosures changes depending on their intention—package, container, carton, urn, jug, pot, vase, bottle, jar, sachet, envelope, wrap, case—they are still, in essence, all different forms of "boxes." Boxes, in fact, are so essential in our society that even containers that serve as "boxes" for other things—cabinets, dressers, attaché cases, briefcases, luggage, sport bags—usually come in their own box. Our homes, the schools we attend, buildings where we work, gyms where we play, auditoriums where we attend events, and concert halls where we listen to wonderful musical performances are also nothing more than big, fancy boxes. The cars, buses, trains, airplanes, subway cars, and most other forms of transportation are little more than winged and/or wheeled boxes.

Boxes, much like almost everything else in our society, also often tend to reflect a sense of status, worth, and value. A diamond ring, for instance—regardless of its size, quality or market worth—quickly loses its mystical glow if presented in a cardboard box. A box seat at a sports arena is deemed extremely more desirable than one that is not "boxed." Precious artwork or an award-winning photograph rapidly dims when displayed in a cheap frame—another form of a box.

Remove the box, and both ourselves and our possessions begin to feel rapidly more vulnerable. A ride in the country on a motorcycle is much more exhilarating than one in a safer automobile. Remove the surround-sound speakers from their precious boxes and their fragility is rapidly exposed. A log cabin in the woods feels more secure than a folding tent, which is a much flimsier type of box. The story of the "Three Little Pigs," in fact, provides testimony to the notion that the stronger the box, the safer we are.

As such, after most of us leave our maternal boxes (i.e., wombs), are born inside of small boxes (i.e., rooms) contained inside of much larger boxes (i.e., hospitals), and transported to our family boxes (i.e., homes) in our transportation boxes (i.e., cars), we are then introduced to our very own box (i.e., bedroom) and placed inside our tinier box (i.e., crib), where we are safe, warm, and secure until we outgrow them, and need a larger box. And in the end, after a life of going from one box to another, most of us end up…in a box (coffin or urn).

SOCIO CULTURAL "BOXES"

The "box notion," then, is one that tends to extend throughout, affect, and often saturate many of our cultural, psychological, social, and educational systems. Persons from certain cultures, for example, are often typecast into stereotypical "boxes" that are thought to reflect any number of personality traits and characteristics. Social status symbols that serve as boxes, such as the type of car one drives and the value of our homes, tend to reflect our apparent wealth and social standing within our community. Although the trends are changing, most schools still follow prescribed educational approaches that revolve around "boxed" formulas that have remained standard, and in many cases even static, over many years. When an idea is introduced that is fresh, new, and innovative, it is often referred to as being "outside the box." Likewise, when a distinctive, creative direction or way of looking at the world or ourselves is suggested, it is also thought of as being "outside the box."

> People with HFA/ASP do not accept current scientific or other views of the world, often rejecting received wisdom and experts in their domains. In this respect they often come across as being childlike and having immature personalities. (Fitzgerald 2004, p.3)

> It would appear that some forms of great creativity can benefit from autistic psychopathology, while "normality"—at least in the statistical sense—produces only replicate ideas. (Fitzgerald 2004, p.57)

Artists, many people think, are those uniquely different people who "think outside the box." Prominent scientists, engineers, architects, designers, and others who approach or reach their conclusions from unusual directions are described as "coming from outside the box." I remember sitting in long, boring, useless meetings listening to conservative, anal compulsive authority figures using transparent strategies they had obviously learned during a "boxed" workshop, perhaps just hours earlier, encouraging us to "look outside the box," for ideas that could give our group the advantage. Whenever any of us came up with such inspired, novel ideas that in fact challenged the existing system and status quo, they were usually either ignored or quickly discarded. It's a good thing that many of the greatest innovators and thinkers who have defined our world throughout the course of history—Einstein, Edison, Descartes, Plato, Socrates, Leonardo da Vinci, Dali, Shakespeare, Mozart, Beethoven, Michelangelo, Picasso, Jules Verne, Coltrane—all chose to ignore boxed recipes.

> We have to give up our conventional non-autistic assumptions and let them teach us about their communication systems in order to build bridges between the two worlds. (Bogdashina 2003, p.20)

> Over my life, I've had trouble with tests because I'm always drawn to consider possible, however remote, situations of the opposite being true—extenuating circumstances, if you like. ("Jean," quoted in J.K. Miller 2003, p.127)

About a decade ago, while just beginning my long apprenticeship into the realms of Asperger's Syndrome, I sat across a ten-year-old boy whose intelligence quotient I was about to assess by using the Wechsler Intelligence Scale for Children (WISC). Before he entered the room, I followed the typical routine I had become accustomed to over the years, removing the briefcase containing the test boxes from my office closet, arranging the furniture in the room, readying the paperwork, and organizing the testing materials in their proper order.

Once my assessment materials were in their customary order I decided to spend the few minutes I had to spare to once again review the information I had received from the school, the boy's parents, and other sources who had attempted to evaluate this young man, all to no avail. The information was confusing and often contradictory, as while he did not seem to fit any particular diagnostic criteria he simultaneously bordered on a number of different profiles. The labels that had been suggested before—Attention Deficit Disorder, Oppositional Defiant Behavior, Conduct Disorder, depression and others—seemed to ring true, but only on the surface. Clearly there was something uniquely different about this troubled little boy.

Upon entering my room, ten-year-old Davey spent a few minutes seemingly quietly scanning everything in the environment with furrowed brow resembling that of a person well beyond his years. His eyes seemed distant yet sharply focused as he appeared to be scrutinizing the office for something that met with his disapproval before he conceded to sitting down. I patiently allowed him to acclimate to the office environment and complete his quiet inspection before inviting him to sit down. After attempting some small talk and describing what the evaluation would generally entail, I began the testing process.

> For autistic people, autism is a way of being...they do not respond in the way we expect them to, because they have different systems of perception and communication...a different set of SPATS—Sense, Perceptions, Abilities and Thinking Systems—that are not in same spectral range as NT individuals...it is wrong to use non-autistic methods to teach and treat autistic children. It is sure to fail and may sometimes even damage their lives. (Bogdashina 2003, p.20)

Davey responded to the first two questions decisively, but with some hesitation, giving the impression that he had better things to do and better places to be at. As I began to ask the third question he politely, but firmly interrupted me with a stern, "Excuse me...but, it appears to me that my parents are paying good money for me to be here and so I don't see why you should be the one who gets to ask the questions. It seems to me that I should be the one asking questions and you should be the one who answers them." In 30 years of clinical work I had never had anyone come up with such an observation. Eventually, as it turned out, I would diagnose Davey with Asperger's Syndrome.

> These people [individuals with autistic spectrum disorder or ADHD] are some of the most exceptional in our world. They are our visionaries, scientists, diplomats, inventors, chefs, artists, writers, and musicians. They are the truly original thinkers—the ones who, even in a corporate environment, think outside the box. They are the people so obsessed with their interests that they are the experts, the scientists, and the architects. In other words, these people are truly a driving force in our culture. (Kennedy 2002, p.147)

After that day, I began to encounter more and more children like Davey, and while there was a common thread that ran across them, they were all still distinctively different. Regardless of the degree of Asperger's Syndrome that was present in these children, adolescents, and adults, their individualities and unique qualities were still filtered through layers of distinct personalities, talents, fears, hopes, intelligence, doubts, self-esteem, anxiety, and myriad other factors that set even the two most identical twins in the world apart from one another.

> When I first started to read about Asperger's Syndrome in preparation for development of my class curriculum, I was struck by the similarities I found between the descriptions of the behavior of people with Asperger's Syndrome and the behavior of several of the most talented actors I worked with in graduate school. Each of these actors possessed a rare and unique way of dealing with the world... That same unique quality gave their performances an exquisite and beautiful ring of truth that cannot be taught. (Davies 2004, pp.4–5)

Still, there was something at their core that was different about their uniqueness. These persons with AS, it quickly became apparent, did not fit into a "box." The WISC, which characteristically comes in a box, just like all other tests that have been designed for evaluating both neurotypical and challenged populations, was obviously not the best choice for this population's unique reality and approach to the world. Other tests I tried encountered similar barriers. It was not that they were resistant, or defensive, "needing to be in control," or oppositional as many suggested, but simply that they just did not seem to fit into any neat, orderly, pre-set standard or mold. In effect, they did not "come in a box."

> A-levels in math were a requirement for a university study in psychology... I studied by identifying precisely what types of mistakes I made. Then I stated these explicitly every time I did sums...my method of study worked. I passed my exam with the highest grade of all 34 students (only 4 passed). ("Darius," a 38-year-old psychology student, quoted in Prince-Hughes 2002, p.38)

Week after week, as more and more of these "different" or "difficult" children marched in and out of my office, I encountered one unique barrier to completing "successful" assessments after another. One would not speak because it was Tuesday, and he did not speak on Tuesdays. Another would not answer questions that began with the letter "D," because he felt that letter was unnecessary. Some could not tolerate one color or another, and so while one who "hated red" would not touch the blocks on one of the subtests, another would not sit on any of the brown furniture because "brown was poo." Many, I later figured out, were simply finding it difficult to concentrate, or remain calm, due to their high levels of sensitivity to a number of sensory stimuli including sounds (voices coming from an adjoining office, rippling water fountain), scents (perfume, cologne, after-shave), and temperature (too hot, too cold), but the primary, and most consistent, culprit appeared to be the fluorescent lights. "The most often reported visual sensitivities are sensitivity to bright light, fluorescent light, colours and certain patterns (especially stripes)" (Bogdashina 2003, p.63).

> I sought out a psychiatrist who claimed to work with adults with Asperger's. I found it odd, when I went to his office, that someone who says they work with AS adults would have so many white walls and fluorescent lights. I already knew I had a limited tolerance for these conditions before reaching overload, so I started off anxious. ("Susan," quoted in J.K. Miller 2003, p.75)

Another child insisted on facing east during our evaluation, and still another would not enter my office because it was "on the left," but he would participate if I simply moved everything to the office across the hall "on the right." A couple of kids refused to do the puzzles, which they claimed were "insulting," or "beneath" them, while others would abruptly, and without warning, indicate they were "done," or would suddenly begin to ask their own questions, tell irrelevant stories, or share data about an obscure topic of interest. Other children would respond to many of my queries in what I would later describe as "video speak," or the voicing of entire scenes and sequences that they had memorized from a book they had read, or movie, television commercial, or program they had watched.

Clearly, these children did not come from a box. Neither the training I had received in graduate school, nor my many years of experience—all of which had come in boxed form—would flow seamlessly with these kids. Stepping *out* of the box, it also became apparent, would also prove futile. The only way that "looking outside the box" yields answers is if the questions came in a box in the first place. Only then can one "step outside" to gain a fresh and creative vantage point.

With these children, the only approach that would work would be one of "no-box." "Autistic children have the ability to see things and events around them from a new point of view, which often shows surprising maturity" (Asperger 1991, p.71).

Perhaps the elemental notion of "the box" is inherent in our very DNAs, the molecular boxes that contain the keys to our very existence.

AS: The No-Box Syndrome

The notion of "no-box" realities is so ephemeral that when one tries to capture it, it becomes much like trying to hold an eyelash in the palm of one's hand in the middle of a windstorm. It just blows away. Although "thinking out of the box" can be conceptualized rather easily by example, trying to capture the "no-box" involves a sizable quantum leap, or detachment, from ordinary reasoning.

By thinking "outside the box," compact discs can be described as containers—or "boxes"—for music, while sheet music serves as "boxes" for melodies, and, taking the "box" idea even further, those melodies can be thought of as "boxes" for the composer's emotions, and the emotions as boxes for life experiences, and so on. Likewise, the same line of reasoning can be stretched to many other things that we do not think of as being "boxed." Books are merely "word boxes"; road signs are "traffic information boxes"; batteries, "energy boxes"; thermometers, "temperature boxes"; pots, "flower boxes"; and picture frames, "photograph boxes." But reading a book is not the same as hearing the stories told, and reading the notes from a musical score pales in comparison to hearing them played by a live orchestra. Much like us, once music and words are freed from their boxes, the spirit comes alive.

> In some autistic people this sense of radical and ineradicable differentness is so profound as to lead them to regard themselves, half jokingly, almost as members of another species…and to feel that autism, while it may be seen as a medical condition, and pathologized as a syndrome, must also be seen as a whole mode of being, a deeply different mode or identity, one that needs to be conscious (and proud) of itself. (Sacks 1995, p.277)

Eventually, I began to approach the children, teens, and adults with AS much like I approached my songwriting. I simply make myself available, with no expectations, no "whys," and no "shoulds, oughts, or musts." After all of the clinical training, professional experience, and countless hours of reading, research, and supervision, I finally understand how one's cumulative life experience at some point just all comes together, and it's all there for us to draw from. Suddenly, the years of martial arts training, songwriting, performing in small venues, working the garden, playing sports and board games, watching movies and TV sitcoms, and daydreaming appear as a tapestry where each of those embroidered threads are no more and no less important than the years spent in school, college, and graduate work.

> My AS strengths include: thinking outside the box, innovating, being persistent, having very good orientation to detail, not being swayed by peer or group pressure, and having a knack for original thought, the ability to work long hours, and a tenacity that can get me through difficult tasks that many would have abandoned. ("Chris," quoted in Stoddart 2005, p.353)

I can now see how the nights I spent slaving over my doctoral dissertation were no more important in the big picture than the nights I have spent infatuated with love or nurturing heartbroken wounds. The countless textbooks I have read and facts I memorized for quizzes, tests, and final exams contained information that, when it comes to understanding myself and others, were no more and no less important than the Batman comics I treasured, or facts I memorized about my favorite baseball players, historical figures, and musicians. The hours I spent over the years listening to, or trying to ignore, my parents, teachers, and others throughout my life have not yielded any wisdom that shines beyond that which I have gained from listening to Beatles' songs or my own heart. In the end, it all just somehow comes together.

An AS/HFA person can think of an NT as a strange person who does not do or say what she/he means, does not see all the peculiar microscopic visual differences around, cannot discriminate visual details and does not behave in a clear, logical way. ("Myriam," a 32-year-old, quoted in Prince-Hughes 2002, p.59)

Data collection

The stories and other information for this book were collected in the following ways:

1. Form A (see Appendix) was included in the manual for my Autism Spectrum Disorders and Asperger's Syndrome workshops sponsored by PESI Health Care, and Health Education Network for a period of 18 months.

2. Forms A and B (see Appendix) were sent via U.S. postal service regular mail, or via e-mail, to a mailing list of workshop participants that was collected over a two-year period.

3. Forms A and B were distributed to persons who indicated they had received a diagnosis of Asperger's Syndrome or high-functioning autism.

4. Forms A and B were made available to parents, teachers, mental health professionals, and others working with persons with Asperger's Syndrome who were interested in distributing those forms to targeted individuals and their families.

5. Personal interviews were conducted with persons who had been diagnosed with Asperger's Syndrome or high-functioning autism.

6. Telephone conversations were conducted with persons who had been diagnosed with Asperger's Syndrome or high-functioning autism.

Research findings, case studies, and other examples from published, peer-reference scientific journals, academic texts, and trade market books are used throughout this book to help balance and further affirm the anecdotal findings, case studies, and other information gathered through the above, more subjective data collection approach. All such supportive evidence is referenced according to standards set by the American Psychiatric Association (APA).

Participants

All of the participants whose stories are related here identified themselves as having been diagnosed with either Asperger's Syndrome or high-functioning autism. Those who self-identified with Pervasive Developmental Disorder, Not Otherwise Specified (PDD–NOS), or simply "autism," were excluded. Information for this book was collected from persons living in all 50 states throughout the United States, as well as several countries in Europe.

The terms *Asperger's Syndrome* (AS) and *high-functioning autism* (HFA) are used throughout this book in accordance with the definitions that correspond to these populations as noted in the fourth edition of the American Psychiatric Association's *Diagnostic Statistical Manual, Text Revision* (DSMIV-TR 2000). The fact that these two labels are sometimes used interchangeably or synonymously by some laypersons and professionals to refer to these two conditions is taken into account for this book. In effect, the primary objective of the book is to identify the characteristics, capabilities, talents, and potential of persons throughout both the AS and HFA spectrums who are of average, or above average, intelligence.

All of the information noted throughout the cases stories in this book are factual as far as they could be authenticated. Identifying information was altered in order to safeguard the privacy of the participants and all information that could have been used to identify particular individuals (specific town, university, family name) was modified. Otherwise, all of the professions noted (engineering, desk clerk, computer technician), and details of sex (male or female), age, grade in school, academic major, and other information, is exactly as it was submitted. In some cases, secondary information such as place of birth or place of current residence was used in cases where the individuals gave permission for those places to be identified. Although the text was edited for grammatical and narrative purposes, great care was taken to preserve the character and personal voice of the participants. Quotes are used throughout to reflect word for word statements and testimonials as spoken, written, or otherwise related by the participants.

What This Book Is *Not*

Part of my motivation for this book was fueled by the recurring themes that I see repeated throughout most of the books that are currently available, the primary topics covered at most seminars and workshops, and typical focus on autism that we see in magazines, newspapers, and many television programs. In short, I am referring to Asperger's Syndrome and autism from the perspective of:

- deficits
- challenges
- impairments
- disorders
- co-morbid conditions
- problems
- difficulties
- weaknesses
- behavior issues
- obstacles
- disadvantages.

Does this mean that persons with AS and HFA do not have any of the above issues? No. Not by any means. "By first grade…David could tell you endless complex stories about superheroes traveling through inter-dimensional portals (Barrett 2003, p. HE1). Although little David's talents were accompanied by many of the deficits typically seen in many persons with AS, that deficit is often balanced with intuitive abilities in areas such as science or art that are beyond most (people)."

Are individuals who fall throughout the AS and HFA spectrums free of challenges, deficits, or impairments? Of course not.

Do they face daily disadvantages? Yes. Most of us can recall a time or two when we were at a disadvantage, or in the minority, so we've all had a fleeting glimpse of how it feels.

Do they have difficulties with social interactions, communication, and reading others? Quite often, yes. After all, how clear do most of us try to make ourselves in the first place? As one of my 14-year-old patients with

AS pointed out to me a couple of years ago, "We don't have the communication problems...*you* have the communication problems!"

Do people with AS and HFA sometimes suffer from "disruptive behaviors," which are also often referred to as "tantrums, rages, or meltdowns"? Don't we all? How many of us can get through a typical day without becoming anxious, sad, annoyed, or stressed? How many of us get through life without ever "losing it"? How long can any of us go before we raise our voice or become emotional over one irritating circumstance or unwarranted provocation?

Are people with AS or HFA confronted with obstacles from internal and external challenges? More often than not. After all, how many of us manage to get through life's challenges without getting in our own way once in a while?

Each of us has personal deficits, vulnerabilities, and weaknesses. At one point or another all of us feel misunderstood, as our minds point one way but our mouths go in a different direction. Depending on the environment, the people we are around, and numerous other life events, we all sometimes come across "challenged," "disordered," or as if we "have a problem." There are many situations when we just don't "fit in," and feel, or come across, as awkward. Have each of us not met a person or two, *not* in the AS/HFA spectrum, who was infuriating? Someone who got on our nerves, exasperated us, maybe by going on and on about a topic we really did not care to hear about? Angered us to the point where we threw a tantrum (either at the moment or shortly afterward)? So why is it that we, the neurotypicals, the mainstream people who lie outside of the very blurry borders of the autism/Asperger spectrums, never labeled?

Why is it, then, that we—those outside of the autistic spectrum—are not also defined according to our "challenges?"

In effect, these topics that focus on "labels of disorder" have been covered thoroughly in literature by now, and they continue to be addressed at workshops, lectures, seminars, and by all facets of the media. So, although challenges for people in "the spectrum" are very, very real, and they are the cause of much suffering, personal struggle, and heartbreak for those individuals, as well as their families, caretakers, friends, relatives, and all of us who care about them and are touched by their lives, the focus of this book is their strengths.

The strengths of AS are those associated with great minds:

- a passionate commitment to an idea

- insight and originality in tackling problems

- tremendous capacity to work to a routine, so essential in any advanced intellectual inquiry

- dogged pursuit of perfection in their chosen areas

- a willingness to forgo opulence and excessive materialism in pursuit of their ideals. (Harpur, Lawlor and Fitzgerald 2003, p.242)

The Book's Focus

This book's focus is to illustrate the strengths, assets, resourceful nature, talents, special qualities, abilities, aptitudes, potential, and promise of persons with AS and HFA. In effect, the objective of this book is to present—through a number of case stories, real-life examples and testimonials from first-person accounts of individuals with AS or HFA, their families or caretakers, close friends or relatives, teachers, therapists or employers—the many ways in which persons with AS and HFA are, have always been, and always will be, invaluable citizens in our world of neurodiversity.

Robert, an eight-year-old fascinated by the Greco-Roman War, is described as astonishing family guests during a dinner party with his prodigious memory by sharing, "the standard spacing of railroad tracks in the United States is based on the original spacing of wheels on an imperial Roman war chariot, which was 4 feet and 8 and one-half inches." His parents are described as encouraging his strengths, and special interests whenever possible, while also entering him in competitive events, such as a spelling bee where he came in second. Likewise, the parents worked closely with their son's teachers, encouraging them to work on his multiplication tables, "which he mastered in a matter of weeks" (Ozonoff, Dawson and McPartland 2002, p.117).

These accounts are respectfully and lovingly presented in Chapter 2—"The Gifts of Asperger's Syndrome"—and Chapter 3—"The World of Gainful Employment." The stories that have been shared for inclusion in this book are also complemented by published examples from peer-referenced journals and books that serve to further illustrate the gifts of persons with AS or HFA. Chapter 4 will look at "Notable Persons with Asperger's Syndrome Phenotypes."

> Prominent individuals who have forever put their mark on history in their respective field might have had the condition described by Hans Asperger... Maybe one could even speculate that historic progress has quite often been made by people with Autism Spectrum conditions. The perseverance, drive for perfection, good concrete intelligence, ability to disregard social conventions, and not worry too much about other people's opinions or critiques, could be seen as advantageous, maybe even a prerequisite for certain forms of new thinking and creativity. (Gillberg 2002, p.134)

The Book's Tone and Purpose

Tony Attwood writes of people with Asperger's Syndrome: "They are a bright thread in the rich tapestry of life. Our civilization would be extremely dull and sterile if we did not have and treasure people with Asperger's Syndrome" (Attwood 1998, p.184).

This book is "Asper-Toned"—AFFIRMATION, STRENGTH, POSITIVITY, EMPOWERMENT, and RESPECT. As such, it is meant to be a constructive, encouraging, and uplifting book aimed at raising awareness, giving hope, and building confidence with regard to the *gifts*, rather than the challenges and deficits, of persons with AS and HFA.

The purpose of this book is to illustrate how, when provided with nurturing, supportive environments, persons with AS and HFA can realize their potentials, live happy, productive lives, and make significant contributions to their families and communities as well as enriching our world and collective consciousness.

> When we were given the diagnosis of AS it was like a gift! I had finally found the reasons for so many things that I just could not figure out. There was a name for this and it came with some strategies for effective support. I was not "crazy," "neurotic," or "crisis-seeking." ("Margot," quoted in Stoddart 2005, p.344)

CHAPTER 2

The Gifts of Asperger's Syndrome

Magical Mystery Michael

> So Alice began telling them her adventures from the time when she first saw the White Rabbit. She was a little nervous about it, just at first, the two creatures got so close to her, one on each side, and opened their eyes and mouths so very wide; but she gained courage as she went on...and then the Mock Turtle drew a long breath, and said, "That's very curious!" (Carroll 1945, p.91)

Even as he gazed around the room as an infant there was an aura about Michael that shone exceptionally bright. What a satisfying windfall it was then to find that a day would not pass by without flurries of unprecedented accounts of his delightful quirkiness. Even as a toddler, so interesting and unusual were his ways of self-expression that one hesitated turning away for fear of missing out on his infinite displays of peculiar wit, odd humor, and eccentric observations.

Before the age of two, Michael knew all of the letters of the alphabet and could arrange letter and number blocks in sequence. Move one out of place and he would rapidly move it back into its rightful position. His ability to assemble puzzles, and decipher pop-up and pull-tab novelty books, was extraordinary enough to astonish even the most persnickety of multigeneration weathered grandmas.

Particularly striking during this very early period of development was Michael's memory. Shortly after turning two years old, Michael began to amaze and amuse everyone in the family by "reading" flash cards. At that point, no one believed that he was actually reading these cards, but—based on his ability for memorization—it was felt that, through summoning his talent for recollection, he was proficiently connecting the words with the pictures on the cards. These feats of "memorization," however, rapidly began to puzzle everyone as he quickly began to point to, and seemingly read, anything that came into view. License plates, car names, logos, traffic signs, labels, words on audio CD and album covers, books for elementary readers, the more he read the more the family argued over whether he could in fact be "reading" or, perhaps even more remarkably, voicing words and symbols he had committed to memory.

One morning, while walking past a newspaper stand with his aunt Melissa, however, the argument was resolutely settled. Pointing to that morning's headline Michael clearly read the words, "Boy's death mystery!" Suddenly, his aunt realized, this was not a line he could have possibly memorized, but one he had just read.

But Michael's cornucopia of surprises did not stop, or even pause, at merely reading and memorization. One morning, after having rapidly assembled a jumbled, multicolored puzzle-map of the United States, he proceeded to identify each state color then name every state and their capitals. Showing flashes of advanced mechanical aptitude during these early years he further dazzled by proficiently assembling Lego and construction type toys that proved frustrating to his older peers. Games that involved identifying shapes, deciphering sequences, mixing and matching, and finding hidden passages appeared to fascinate him. Once a way around a task within his sphere of talent had been resolved, it seemed, the "solution code" would rapidly be committed to memory.

But how exceptional, exactly, was his memory? One afternoon, while on a walk around his grandmother Iris's townhouse complex, I casually mentioned to the precocious three-year-old that he was starting to look "very grown up." Without hesitation, he replied, "If it had grown up, she said to herself, it would have made a dreadfully ugly child—but it makes rather a handsome pig, I think."

Although, by now, many of us in the family had grown accustomed to Michael's unpredictable, off-the-cuff remarks this one seemed not only particularly strange, but strangely recognizable. As soon as we returned home I wrote his exact words down and kept rereading them throughout the evening in an effort to identify where I had heard them before. Later that night, I walked into Michael's room to tuck him into bed and found him reading an old copy of Lewis Carroll's *Alice's Adventures in Wonderland*. Immediately, I realized I had stumbled upon the source of Michael's mysterious quote from earlier that afternoon. As soon as he fell asleep, I slipped back into the room and stole away with the book, hastily reading it in search of the actual passage. A while later, on page 56, there it was, word for word, just as Michael had voiced it earlier that evening. My random question had somehow triggered his astonishing memory, cueing him to respond with a line from a book he was currently reading and had obviously memorized.

This seemed to me both sensational and impossible. How could such a young child, struggling as he was at that age to use pragmatic language, not only memorize such a complex line, but be able to contextually cue it to a question about being "grown up?" As Michael's feats of reading and memorization surfaced we all continued to fine-tune our awareness to his idiosyncrasies. The more we tuned in, the more his pearls of giftedness became apparent.

Once, during Christmas holidays as the family gathered around the tree preparing for a sing-a-long, someone suggested we try our hand at the "Twelve Days of Christmas." After struggling over a few bars, we quickly realized that none of us had a firm grasp on the actual lyrics. No one, that was, except for four-year-old Michael who in no short measure let us all know that he had the words down pat. Finding a white board and marker, Michael and I retreated to a quiet room where I could jot down the words as he dictated them. As I struggled to keep up with his rapid transcription, however, I accidentally made a smudge mark in mid-sentence. Immediately, Michael became quite exasperated and shouted, "No comma! No comma!" while pointing at my innocent grammatical transgression.

At first, forgetting for a moment that I was responding to a four-year-old, I tried to explain to him that this wasn't a comma, but, in fact, just a guiltless mark. Unimpressed, he swiftly interrupted me repeating his firm command. "No comma! No comma!" he reiterated admonishingly. There would be no further transcription until the splotch-comma was removed from the page.

"How can this kid know punctuation?" I thought to myself, as I wet the tip of my thumb and duly corrected my faux-pas.

By the time that Michael enrolled in the first grade, at the age of six, his reading and spelling scores were both at the top of the gifted range of ability. Likewise, his knowledge of many of the topics that are often typical of children with Asperger's—dinosaurs, cars, weather markers, pop culture, U.S. presidents, astronomy, geography, geographical markers—easily lived up to the "little professor" moniker by which children with AS are endearingly known. His ability to memorize extended passages from movie scripts, book passages, song lyrics (he could sing karaoke songs after one performance without further need for the words) and, more impressively, actually be able to understand, and communicate his wealth of knowledge, never ceased to impress even the harshest skeptics. In second grade, when his teacher was reviewing the "seven colors of the spectrum," and named them, he raised his hand and asked, "What about fuchsia and chartreuse?"

During fourth grade, Michael's teachers reported that, during recess, his topics of discussion included feudal England, Imperial China's Dynasties, the state's topography, and a slave's rights to habeas corpus. During his "meteorology period" the teacher reported that his classmates often turned to Michael, rather than the encyclopedia, for information regarding topics such as the differences between typhoons and hurricanes, the connection between earthquakes and tsunamis, and the different types of cloud formations. It was around this time that I fondly recall his aunt Roz and I sitting with Michael at a clinic as he awaited his evaluation and watched him briskly flip through a stack of *Where's Elmo?* books adroitly pointing to the hidden main character in page after dizzying page. Being a clinician myself, I could barely contain my impish thoughts as I previewed the unprecedented challenge that Michael's unsuspecting evaluator would soon be facing.

Comfortably balancing his intellectual talents Michael's sense of "AS" humor also often springs up in most colorful, verbally witty ways. During fifth grade, when placed in a time-out after an argument with his teacher, Michael pleaded his case by stating, "I can't take this incarceration…what do I need to do to end this torment? I'll do anything to be freed from this desolation; I'll even eat my vegetables!" The following year, confronted with a problem in sixth-grade honor's math class—a relative strength but not in par with his superior verbal abilities—his assessment of the task ahead was, "I'll never be able to finish this…it's going to be just like Mozart's *Requiem*!" A year later, while in seventh grade, Michael was challenged by his teacher to teach a section in his social studies class, prepare and administer a quiz to his peers, and then grade the papers. Realizing how this "taste of power" had temporarily clouded his judgment during his strict grading of his colleague's papers, he dejectedly reported his self-disappointment by uttering, "Why did I allow the power to turn me into a Napoleon?!"

An avid social studies and history buff, Michael is the ultimate companion during holiday visits to historical landmarks. While on site at Washington, D.C.'s Lincoln memorial at the age of 11, for instance, he awed a tour group by reciting the entire Gettysburg address by heart while standing at the entrance and staring out into the open mall. A few hours later, while visiting the hall of presidents, he received a roaring applause from a large crowd after standing in the center of a room and delivering one of President Roosevelt's speeches from memory.

The following summer, during a trip to historic Gettysburg, Michael promptly seized the moment when the tour guide offered his initial question as a challenge to the tour group of children, teenagers and adults.

No sooner had the words; "Is there anyone here who could tell me who Edward Everett was?" left the guide's lips, than Michael's elated hand sprung up jubilantly. "Senator Everett, a member of the Whig party, was a representative from Massachusetts and he was the principal speaker at the dedication of the cemetery on November 19, 1863," he indicated, "but although his speech went on for over two hours it was forever overshadowed by Lincoln's two-minute Gettysburg address, and the rest is history. As author Garry Wills wrote, 'Senator Everett's oration will live, now, as the foil to that better thing that followed'!"

"How old are you son?" asked the impressed tour guide. "Twelve," answered Michael. "And what grade are you in?" the man followed up. "Seventh Grade," Michael proudly replied. As the rest of the tour group stared, notably impressed, the guide added, "You young man, will go far!" Throughout the remainder of that tour Michael ably answered every other question posed to the group, at one point even correcting the tour guide on an obscure fact, a display which prompted the trained expert to remove his guide's cap and place it on Michael's head.

As of this writing, Michael is just beginning eighth grade where he is enrolled in gifted classes. Upon telling him that a section in this book would be about him his pressing question was whether his story would help others to better understand those with AS. When I described the cover of the book to him over the telephone, I mentioned that it would feature his picture, surrounded by an aura of fractals.

"Do you know what fractals are, Michael?" I asked sincerely, as I know that his current, primary interests such as history, social studies, civics, and others are far removed from quantum physics and mathematics. "I think so," was his typically modest reply. "Aren't they colorful geometric figures that are like the mathematical representation of chaos theory?"

"How can this kid know about fractals?" I thought to myself, as I smiled and shook my head.

And so, at the age of 13, the gift of Michael continues to impress.

She pictured to herself how this same little sister of hers would, in the af-ter-time, be herself a grown woman; and how she would keep, through all her riper years, the simple and loving heart of her childhood; and how she would gather about her other little children, and make their eyes bright and eager with many a strange tale, perhaps even with the dream of Won-derland of long ago; and how she would feel with all their simple sorrows, and find a pleasure in all their simple joys, remembering her own child-life, and the happy summer days. (Carroll 1945, p.112)

———

THE GIFTS OF ASPERGER'S SYNDROME

Carlton the Gift Giver

As they each took their turns going around the room, telling their class-mates all about their plans for summer vacation, Mrs. Remington's fourth-graders were also to take this opportunity on their last day of school to present their class a "gift" for which they had been given one week to prepare. As it had been explained one week earlier, the "gift" was to be a gesture, such as a general wish, something personal, a poem, or a passage from a book that could serve as end of the year closure and be offered as a fond farewell.

In a way, the exercise was to serve as a school year "bookend" to com-plement an assignment that children had all taken part in during the first day of school many months earlier. On that day in early September, the children had been asked to name their "ten ideals," and were given the cat-egories of a favorite color, song, movie, musician, type of animal, television show, sports team, place they would most want to visit, type of car, and favorite fruit. After that day, no one in the class, including the teacher, had likely given much thought to that assignment. After all, the activity had been meant mostly as a relationship-building exercise to help the students to feel a little more comfortable with themselves and their classmates. Carlton, however, had not forgotten. On this final day of school in June, when his turn arrived to share his "gift" with the class, Carlton stood up, reached down beside of his desk and picked up a large box.

Carrying the box around the room, he approached each student, and the teacher, wished them a "splendid summer," and handed out the follow-ing: three cassette tapes each containing a song (by Green Day, Usher, and Nelly), a map of Italy and one of the Rocky Mountains, a small moon globe, two movie posters (*The Incredibles* and *Spiderman 2*), a poster featur-ing all of the Simpson characters, a promotional button for *Star Wars, Episode III: Revenge of the Sith*, three baseball stickers (Boston Red Sox, Balti-more Orioles, and Florida Marlins), five magazine pictures (Chris Rock, Ben Stiller, Johnny Depp, Jim Carrey, and Jennifer Alva), one Red Deli-cious apple and one kiwi fruit, three car pictures cut out from a magazine (P.T. Cruiser convertible, Hummer, and Corvette), and six Polaroid pictures (a horse, two cats, two dogs, and an iguana). As it had happened many times before, Carlton, who has Asperger's Syndrome, had apparently not clearly understood the exercise or the teacher's instructions. But his sensational memory, also by now legendary among his classmates, had not failed him.

Each gift, the teacher realized, reflected each of his classmates' "ten personal ideals." "To cure someone of AS would be to take away their personality and some really cool abilities too." (Jackson 2002, p.36).

Twelve-year-old Sameer, who rarely made mention of anything personal during his therapy sessions, handed his therapist a wrinkled paper bag...obviously he had noticed the type of pen she used, remembered the single occasion she had mentioned her music tastes, and registered which snacks she occasionally left sitting on her desk. There in the bag, which he had taped closed and labeled "JA" in black marker, were her favorite model of pen, filled with ink in her favorite color; a bag of her favorite type of potato chip; and a homemade CD containing her favorite song—recorded 50 times... Janice could see from his beaming face as she thanked him that this was a hugely satisfying accomplishment for this boy with Asperger's Syndrome. (Ozonoff *et al.* 2002, p.114)

The Death Ray

On his first day at a new school seven-year-old Nelson entered the classroom and almost immediately informed his teacher that he could not "bear withstanding the debilitating death rays bombarding the room." Over the next few days, Nelson's constant bickering about the "death rays" created ample disruption within the class, prompting the teacher to send him first to the principal's office for discipline and later to visits with the school's counselor for therapy. Regardless of what the school came up with, attempts to have Nelson sit in the room failed day after day. He would begin to moan (to "keep the debilitating noises from melting my brain"), cover his ears (to "keep out the debilitating vibrations"), or flail his hands and arms wildly (to "shake off the debilitating rays").

> Children with AS may also have visual oversensitivities that are difficult for others to comprehend. For example, Nicole cannot concentrate or work in a room that has fluorescent lighting. She says that she can see the light pulsating and that the movement is very disrupting and hurts her eyes. (Myles *et al.* 2002, p.32)

> Fluorescent lights, which are common in schools and workplaces, can be bothersome because they tend to flicker. The SD [sensory disordered] person notices the flickering long before most others do. (Huebner 2001, p.474)

As soon as it one could be scheduled, a consult was held between Nelson's parents and the school's psychologist, nurse, doctor, teacher, and principal. The meeting, however, yielded no mutually agreed upon way of dealing with Nelson's "irrational" behaviors, as opinions for why Nelson was acting in this irrational manner ranged from "poor parenting," to "control issues," to "chemical imbalance," to his simply being a "spoiled brat." The school decided to refer him to an outside professional for a more extensive evaluation. The very following Monday, however, Nelson brought to school a printout that warned about "the harms of fluorescent lights" that he had downloaded from the Internet and shared it with his teacher. "This," the little boy insisted, was the "source of danger" that permeated the classroom. That evening, after getting permission from the school principal, Nelson's teacher approached the same website from where Nelson had downloaded his information and placed a rush order, using her own money, for a set of full-spectrum bulbs and a kit to make the light fixtures in her classroom adaptable to the new bulbs. Nelson was excused from coming to class until the bulbs arrived and were properly installed.

Once the new bulbs were in place, Nelson returned to school. Entering the now full-spectrum lit classroom, Nelson cautiously walked into the room, looked around, and calmly took his seat.

"How do you feel, Nelson?" his teacher asked. "The death rays have been overcome," he responded.

Since the nine weeks when the full-spectrum bulbs were installed, Nelson has not missed a single day of class, and his concern about the "debilitating rays" is now a thing of the past.

By the way, the consultation with the outside professional was cancelled three days after Nelson's successful return to the classroom.

> Fluorescent light has been reported by many autistic individuals to be very difficult to tolerate, because they can see a 60-cycle flicker. Problems with flickering can range from excessive eyestrain to seeing a room pulsate on and off. (Bogdashina 2003, p.63)

Suelan's Leaky Link

One fall day Suelan arrived home from school and suddenly stopped in her tracks, pouted, and began to walk around the house not saying a word and displaying a very concerned look on her face. Since Suelan often showed "unusual behaviors," particularly after hectic and stressful school days, her parents had grown accustomed to having her act "a little different" once in a while. On this day, however, as Suelan calmly walked around each room, she walked carefully and continually smelled the air in a slow, almost rhythmic pattern. Suelan's mother, who quietly followed her around during this curious display, described the behavior much like "a cat that knows there is a mouse lurking somewhere around."

Eventually, Suelan's nose—otherwise known around family circles as her "sensory radar"—led her to the basement, and the downstairs laundry area. There, Suelan, now moving more rapidly, quickly found her way to a corner where pipes connected to an outside gas container that fueled the home's furnace. "Right there," Suelan said as she pointed to the copper tubing, "right there is the leaky link!"

Having said that, the little girl turned to her mother and instructed her to "call the furnace company without hesitation!" When the furnace company's answering service indicated that it was after hours and they could only come during an emergency, the mother asked Suelan how much gas she felt was leaking from the pipes. "It's nearing a lethal level!" replied the little girl. After relating this to the furnace company's operator, which felt the mother was being oversensitive, the latter insisted that this could in fact be an actual emergency and indicated she would pay the extra fee if she were proven wrong.

A couple of hours later, during which time Suelan insisted that all family members and pets "remain outside of the house," the repair man finally arrived and examined the pipe. His diagnosis? The leak in the pipe was in fact coming from a loosely fitting joint and the amount of gas that was entering their home was, in fact, quite toxic, posing a significant danger to anyone in the house. Impressed by the little girl's ability to actually sense the actual source of the gas leak, the repair man asked the mother how her young daughter had been able to pinpoint the spot with such accuracy. The mother, by now used to her daughter's array of extraordinary abilities, proudly responded, "She has Asperger's Syndrome!"

Some autistic individuals have olfactory sensitivities comparable to canines. (Bogdashina 2003, p.54)

It Takes a Thief

Returning home after a weekend away in the mountains, the Cabrera family noticed that a number of large items were missing. Before long, they realized that their home had been ransacked during their absence. Within hours, a policeman arrived at their home and began to gather information. The family was promptly informed by the officer that the possibility of actually catching the perpetrator and recovering their possessions was, at best, a very long shot.

As if news could not get any worse, a few hours later the insurance adjuster assessed the losses and shared the news that, under their plan, unless the family had detailed descriptions of their stolen property, including date and place of purchase, and actual costs, they would be unable to reimburse them for their losses. Without hesitation, 12-year-old Stephen, who had been quietly sitting on his favorite spot at the family bay window, interrupted. "The loot," he said, "consisted of the following…" Over the next few minutes, Stephen proceeded to list, in detail, each and every item missing from the household.

Included in his detailed information Stephen noted:

- a Sony Handycam CCD TRV308 Camcorder with ¼ inch CCD imager with 320K Pixels, 20X optical with 460X digital zoom lens and digital zoom interpolation

- a Sony UPD2500 Digital color photo printer with high print quality at 310 dpi resolution that is both PC and Mac compatible

- a Nikon F5 35mm SLR camera with 1005 pixel 3D color matrix metering, three built-in exposure meters, and 3D multi-sensor balanced fill flash

- a Dimension 8400 Dell desktop computer with Intel Pentium 4 Processor 550 with HT Technology, 512MB Dual Channel and 80GB hard drive, a 16X DVD-ROM Drive, Sound blaster and Dell 5650 Surround Sound 5.1 speaker system, which came with a Dell A960 printer

- an Inspiron 5150 Mobile Intel Pentium 4 laptop computer with 2.80GHz, Windows XP, and 15-inch TFT display, 256MB DDR SDRAM, 30 GB hard drive, and 8X DVD-ROM drive

- a 32-inch Sony Trinitron XBR 37 rear-projection color TV

- a 27-inch Sony Trinitron flat screen Wega TV
- a Hallicrafters, "White Face" SX 71 Ham Shortwave radio, fully restored, with 13 tube, double conversion circuit—a real beauty!
- a Sony TA-AX44 Integrated stereo legato linear amplifier
- a Pioneer Cassette Deck, CT-S405
- a Phillips CDR-785 3 disk audio CD player/recorder
- a Sony p, Ix-240 turntable
- a Panasonic SC-PM39D, five-disc, DVD portable stereo system, etc.

After his initial shock, the insurance adjuster actually asked Stephen to slow down, back up, and begin reciting all of this information so that he could write it down. In the end, the adjuster was so impressed with Stephen's detailed recollections of every stolen item that he assured the family he would take responsibility for the accuracy of the child's statements and would take it upon himself to look up the book value for all of the missing items. After a few weeks, although the thief remained at large and "the loot" had not been recovered, the family received a check that covered the major part of their losses.

At the age of two, David was described as "so smart, it's almost scary. He concentrates so hard on what he's doing that you can't distract him from it." By age three "he knew by heart the license plate numbers of all our neighbors within a two-block radius. By four, he'd memorized detailed plot lines from books and videos, and would recite them... Halfway through kindergarten David could read as well as many kids in the upper grades." (Barrett 2003, p. HE1)

The Official Reader

On his second birthday, Carson's dad picked him up off the floor, and stood him up on the chair at the head of the family's festively decorated dinner table. Around the table, Carson's family members—including his mother, father, two older brothers and younger sister—various relatives, neighbors, and friends stood ready to sing to the cherubic-faced child only the second birthday song of his young life. Directly in front of Carson, a number "2" candle sat atop the delicately ornamented, triple-layered chocolate cake. "Blow out the candles!" demanded his oldest brother. "And make a wish!" Before following his brother's advice, however, Carson, did what came naturally. "Happy Birthday, Carson!" he read, phonetically deciphering the words written across the top of his birthday cake. Amazed by the little munchkin's precocious gift of reading, the entire room exploded in a raucous applause.

> As far back as I can remember, I have had thoughts and ideas which, at the time, seemed to make me unique. In actual fact many of my earliest memories are theories I have about the world around me. Perhaps my earliest thoughts were about phonetics. Without actually knowing what "phonetics" meant and probably not even knowing the alphabet, I was able to think to myself that "P" was a harder version of "b" as was "T" to "d", "K" to "g" and "S" to "z." This all worked reasonably well inside my own head, but at the time I was only four. (Jacobs 2003, p.99)

> My boy is classic Asperger's. He knows everything about everything. He has always read the encyclopedia in every free moment because he thinks it is fun. ("Mary," quoted in Miller 2003, p.119)

Seven years later, Carson's parents went on their weekly drive, taking their nine-year-old lover of words to the county's nursing home where they go to volunteer their services. For four hours each Friday night, young Carson makes the rounds across the third floor—three being his favorite number—reading a variety of books to the residents housed at this geriatric facility. The feedback from the nursing home residents is unanimously positive, with many of them stating that each time that this young, hyperlexic boy with Asperger's Syndrome walks into their room it brings them "new life." Carson religiously spends 20 minutes reading to each resident. During his initial visit with a new resident, Carson always asks if there is any particular book that he or she would like for him to read. Novels, westerns, action-adventures, comics, mystery thrillers, religious, professional, or technical, Carson has read them all. Sometimes, however, after a few visits, many of the residents insist that he bring along one of his own favorites. So enamored are they by his readings that most insist on no one else continuing "Carson's books" unless it's him and so, each Friday night, the young boy picks up exactly at the point where he left off the week before.

When asked if he enjoys spending Friday nights reading to the elderly in nursing homes, Carson simply replies that there is no better way to spend time than reading. Besides, he adds, this gives him "the excuse" to read books that he might not otherwise get to in his own time. When asked about his favorite book of all time, Carson's reply is, "Whichever one I am reading at the moment."

> I have always been an avid reader, and I am driven to take in more and more information to add to my video library. A severely autistic computer programmer once said that reading was "taking in information." For me, it is like programming a computer. (Grandin 1995, p.38)

The Disciplinarian

Ten-year-old Tevin claims he would like to be a "disciplinarian" when he grows up. When asked if he knows what that means, he replies, "Well, of course. A disciplinarian is one who exudes authority and commands obedience or else."

Fair enough. But let's take a closer look at what he actually means.

An incident that took place just days before this story was related to me by Tevin's grammar teacher helps to shed some light regarding his notion of "discipline," allowing us to better appreciate his understanding of the term.

Twice each year, Tevin's school holds practice fire drills. Knowing about his Asperger-related auditory sensory issues, precautions were taken prior to the year's initial fire-safety exercise. A few days prior to the day when the fire drill would take place, Tevin was called into the school counselor's office and gently informed about the procedure that would take place on the following day. During the briefing, he was told exactly at what time the alarms would sound, explained they would be quite loud, that the noise would last for a fairly long period of time, and that the exercise would likely create a fair amount of chaos and additional chatter among the children. He was then given the option of (a) staying home that day, (b) "hanging out" with the school counselor or any other teacher of his choice during the exercise, or (c) riding it out. His response was "It seems it's my responsibility as a disciplinarian to make sure that all goes well." Again, fair enough.

On the next day however, when the children were being escorted out as dictated by the fire department procedures, Tevin refused to follow the prescribed pattern. When the teachers tried to convince him to join the group he indicated that "it would be suicide" to follow that route, and insisted there was "a better way." Over the past few days, he had taken it upon himself to make "a detailed visual blueprint of the environment" and thus refused to comply with the school's "disastrous, archaic rules" of fire safety and mode of exiting the building.

The issue, however, did not end there. Over the next few days Tevin would simply not let the matter drop. He held meetings with the school counselor, assistant principal, and even the school janitor, showing them his schema for an "enhanced escape route." They all humored him for a while, but always ended up with the notion that the fire department probably knew best what routes were the safest and most practical.

A few weeks later, just before the July 4th holiday, the local fire marshal came to the school to offer a "fire-safety lecture." During the assembly, Tevin stood up in front of the entire student body and confronted the fire chief about his "archaic and death-inviting exit routes." Although the confrontation yielded a hearty roar from the student body, the fire marshal politely humored Tevin by inviting him to spend a few moments after the assembly so that they could discuss his concerns in private. Tevin accepted the offer.

After the assembly, fire chief and disciplinarian accompanied the assistant principal into her office. There, Tevin took out his blueprints, one for the "enhanced escape route," which had by now been further improved by adding colors and clearer graphics, and one depicting the school's "barbaric route," dramatically enlivened by graphic scenes depicting children and teachers in flames and parents on their knees screaming and crying outside of the burning building. As he examined Tevin's well-detailed diagrams the fire marshal became very pensive. He took the diagrams and asked both Tevin and the assistant principal to accompany him. Making his way down the school corridors guided by Tevin's diagrams, the fire marshal scribbled notes while murmuring to himself. After completing both routes, first Tevin's, then the school's, he asked if he could speak with the assistant principal for a few moments and asked Tevin to wait outside of the latter's office.

After a few minutes, the two adults asked Tevin to join them inside the office, at which time they both shook the young boy's hand and congratulated him on an exceptional job. As it turned out, Tevin had been right all along. His route would cut several minutes off during an evacuation, minimize congestion, avoid two potential traffic jams, and lead to a much smoother coordination of efforts throughout the school.

When asked how it was that he was able to come up with his superior scheme, Tevin merely replied, "It's my special brain, that's all, it's just very disciplined."

> I figured out he sees a lot of things normal people can't see. He seems to care about and hear very small things that others do not perceive… He sees things in print that I cannot see. (Stephen Shore's wife, Yi Liu, describing her husband; Shore 2003, p.107)

> With collected energy and obvious confidence and, yes, with a blinkered attitude towards life's rich rewards, they go their own way, the way to

which their talents have directed them from childhood. Thus, the truth of the old adage is proved again: good and bad in every character are just two sides of the same coin. It is simply not possible to separate them, to opt for the positive and get rid of the negative. We are convinced, then, that autistic people have their place in the organism of the social community. (Asperger 1991, p.89)

Vaschel the Liberator

For about a year now, 11-year-old Vaschel had been taking his weekly allowance and spending it on "something private." At first, his parents felt that affording him their ultimate trust and privacy was essential. However, after a while, and after discussing this issue with a number of friends and relatives who shared horror stories about "what children are doing nowadays," Vaschel's parents began to get concerned.

Could it be drugs? Cigarettes? Liquor? Porn? Was their young son being taken advantage of by other children, or bullied into giving away his money? Could there be an adult involved who was abusing, exploiting, terrorizing, or otherwise harming the boy? One afternoon, they decided to confront him. Regardless of various attempts and strategies by the parents, however, Vaschel refused to talk and the matter was temporarily dropped.

One Saturday morning, however, Vaschel's father decided to follow the boy. Vaschel always received his allowance on Friday evenings, and so his father suspected that Saturday was the day when he might be spending it.

A very anxious and guilt-ridden father followed his son as he rode his bicycle down to the town center. There, he watched his son dismount his bicycle and enter the local grocery store. The father parked outside of the store, keeping his distance, and waited. After a few moments, Vaschel came out carrying two large, obviously heavy bags that he carefully placed inside of the two baskets that sat astride the rear of his bicycle. Vaschel's father watched curiously and cautiously continued to follow the boy to his next destination.

A few minutes later, Vaschel arrived at the town's local animal shelter, just a few blocks away. He dismounted his bike, removed the two bags and entered the shelter. About half an hour later, Vaschel's father decided to enter the building as his curiosity had by now exceeded his patience. Inside, he introduced himself as Vaschel's father and demanded to know what was going on.

The receptionist shared a broad smile, shook Vaschel's father's hand, and complimented him on being an exceptional parent. She indicated she knew Vaschel well and that everyone at the shelter was quite impressed with him. She then asked if he could wait a moment as she called the shelter's supervisor whom she felt would want to meet "Vaschel's father."

Within a couple of minutes, a young man walked out to the lobby and greeted the father again, exhibiting a hearty grin. "Your son is an exceptional young man," the shelter's manager stated. "You must be very proud. The world would be a much better place if there were more children like him and adults like yourself sharing such an excellent example for their children."

Vaschel's father stood perplexed. He was happy that everyone at this shelter knew his son, and were so impressed with him, but he still had no idea why this was so. After thanking the young manager for his compliments regarding both his son and himself, Vaschel's father explained that he had no idea what they were talking about or what his son was doing there.

The manager laughed and stated that, judging from Vaschel's exceptionally quiet, shy demeanor, he was not surprised that the young boy's relationship with the shelter was a secret. As it turned out, over the past few months, Vaschel had been coming up to the shelter and bringing bags of animal food that he donated on a regular basis. Once there, he would spend a couple of hours with the animals, petting and playing with them with great delight. Although he would characteristically remain quiet around the people there, he seemed to "glow as soon as he came in contact with the animals." "Your son," the young manager added, "has a special magic when it comes to animals. Even the ones who shy away from the workers, or cower in the corners when greeted, seem to feel completely comfortable with him. There is something about Vaschel that makes the animals feel safe."

Asked if he wanted to watch his son in action, Vaschel's father quickly indicated that he would prefer to keep his visit there a secret. Although the boy would certainly understand his parent's looking out for him by following him to the shelter, the father felt that this knowledge would also place doubt in his son's mind as to the level of trust that his parent's afforded him. Renewed with pride, trust, and confidence in his young son, Vaschel's father smiled all the way home.

> I have had a special love of animals all my life. I spent a lot of time around animals as I was growing up, showing horses at 4-H fairs, helping my aunt with her livestock on her ranch. I don't think I am unusual in my love of animals and feel that many of us on the autism spectrum are attuned to their ways. That is why working as a veterinary technician or assistant is such a great job for many of us. ("Jane," a veterinary assistant and technician, quoted in Grandin and Duffy 2004, p.138)

> Tenderness was his greatest gift, although it lay beyond his recognition. It was the unconscious tenderness of a small child. (Jacobs 2003, p.55)

Evan the Incomparable

On my drive to a local high school to evaluate a young man who had been described as, "a weird kid who's probably on drugs or up to something," I spotted, to my left, a couple of boys struggling uphill as a light, steady rain fell upon them. They looked exhausted and miserable. About a hundred or so yards ahead, a slightly larger group of boys, six or seven of them, came into view. As I passed them, driving slowly as I neared the school zone, I noticed their rain-soaked hair, faces, and bodies huffing and puffing their way up the steep incline. A bit further, a couple of hundred yards or so, a larger group of boys, this bunch so far the most athletic looking of the lot, ran rhythmically along what was now almost level ground. I drove on. A few moments later, quite a distance ahead of the closest group of runners, I spotted one final lone runner about one-quarter mile up the road. "This must be the star of the track team," I thought to myself, and, as I drove past him, I slowed down to get a good look at him, unable to resist giving him the thumbs up.

Arriving at the school, I found my way to the school counselor's office, reviewed the case with the counselor, and readied the room for the evaluation. The counselor stepped out indicating he would go to "fetch the boy" for me. A few minutes later, I was surprised to see none other than my supposed track star.

"Are you the young man I just saw leading the pack out in that rain?" I asked. "What pack?" he asked, painfully struggling to make eye contact. "The group of boys running up the hills toward the school" I clarified. "Oh," he replied. I stood, waiting patiently for a few seconds expecting a lengthier response.

"Well…" I asked after a sustained, uncomfortable silence, "was that you…running ahead of the whole group?"

"I am on the track team," he replied.

"Looks to me like you *are* the track team," I responded, trying to elicit some sort of emotion from the young man.

"No, that's impossible," he answered back, looking at me through the corner of his eye, "one person can't be a team."

"Yes, you are right," I responded, realizing he was totally serious, "but it seemed to me that you are the fastest one on the whole team."

"Yes, I am," he replied, again without further elaboration.

"What do you think makes you so fast?" I asked, partly trying to establish an initial, working relationship, and partly out of sheer curiosity. After a few moments of deep pensive processing, the young boy answered, "Well, in this school, there are 16 boys on the track team. There are 15, plus me, and that's 16. And of all the boys, I run the fastest."

His response, short, simple, and to the point, lacked any hint of conceit, aggrandizement, or elaboration.

"What do you think about when you run?" I asked, now trying to move closer to a line of questions that would steer us closer toward our evaluation.

"When I run," he replied, "I don't think of anything except what's in my mind, which is nothing. And so the best time is while I run, the longer the better."

"What happens when you get tired?"

"I don't get tired."

"That's pretty amazing," I responded. "You must be in fantastic shape."

"Yes, I am," he replied, again, completely void of any sense of arrogance or pretense.

"When I run," I shared, "I usually get tired pretty quickly, and I get a pain on my side. Do you ever get a pain on your side?"

Beginning to look somewhat uncomfortable by my ongoing questions, he sighed heavily and responded, "I don't get tired and I don't get a pain on my side, and I don't run out of breath."

At that moment, I realized I had not formally introduced myself to Evan, nor given him the courtesy of allowing him to introduce himself to me. Having done so, we then moved on to the formal evaluation. A couple of hours later, having completed the assessment that would later support my initial notion that this spectacular young runner had a diagnosis of high functioning autism, I bid farewell to Evan and left the school.

As I walked across the parking lot to my car I knew that Evan was neither "weird," on drugs, or "up to anything." In fact, I had just had the good fortune of spending some quality time with a unique individual who had a very special talent and almost superior ability to excel at distancing himself from the rest of the pack.

During my early adolescence, I discovered that I had a talent for running. Soon I gained the respect of other runners and my peers for my running ability. I felt included as part of the running group at my school. I also enjoyed the social status that my achievement in running brought me...

Through running, I was going to prove to others and myself that not only was I worthy as a person, but I was capable of success… Running was my self-esteem, my identity, and my purpose, and it gave me validity as a person. ("Donna," quoted in Stoddart 2005, p.337)

The Community Patriot

Following the tragedy that is now generally referred to as "9/11," the United States experienced resurgence in national pride and unity. Part of the collective effort to demonstrate the nation's camaraderie has included an unprecedented display of American flags. Unfortunately, many well-meaning persons intent on expressing their support by raising the ole "Stars and Stripes" in all its glory forgot that, as it is with most things, there are a number of rules that must be followed. Fortunately, any community worth its salt in national pride has its fair share of children with Asperger's Syndrome to lead the way.

> Their [persons with Asperger's Syndrome] qualities of personality include being honest, loyal, reliable, forthright, and having a strong moral code and sense of justice. Their cognitive qualities include an exceptional memory, enthusiasm and knowledge about their special interest, an original way of thinking, good imagination and remarkable ability to think using pictures. These qualities are not unique to the syndrome but are enhanced by it. (Attwood 1998, p.179)

A few months after 9/11 nine-year-old Tyler, himself a proud resident of a small, gated community in the north east, took it upon himself to become his neighborhood's "flag police." Each evening over the period of a week or so, unbeknown to his parents, little Tyler would gather up his "flag enforcement" kit, its contents meticulously organized in his special briefcase. The "kit" included a notepad, flashlight, extra batteries, his Nemo watch, a whistle, two candy bars, a water bottle, a sheet of adhesive gold stars, and, for some inexplicable reason, a picture of Don Quixote and a toy sailboat. He would then slip on his favorite blue windbreaker and march his way around the neighboring community delivering the "politically correct flag gospel." Tyler's "flag kit" also contained copies of a document he had downloaded from the Internet called "How to Display the Flag."

Stopping at each home displaying a flag, Tyler would knock on the front door or ring the doorbell. If no one answered, he would leave a note indicating that he would return on the following night at the same time. Whenever someone did respond, Tyler would either commend them on their "proper display of the flag," and award them a gold star, or give them a short lecture on the "proper way to display the American flag." In the latter case, the lecture would be followed by (a) a warning, (b) the admonition that "a citation would be given" if the proper actions were not taken to correct the situation, and (c) a copy of the document. At that point Tyler would simply bid farewell, turn around, and continue on with his mission.

It took a full week before word of their patriotic son would reach his parents. Most in the community simply felt that Tyler's parents were, certainly, hiding just out of sight and keeping an eye on their little boy whom they had "obviously" prepared, trained, and sent out on this mission. The little boy, undoubtedly, was just the parents' "cute" way to get their message across without rousing a defensive reaction from their neighbors.

Once word reached Tyler's parents about his exploits they could not understand how he was able to sneak away, every night, in order to complete his rounds. All along, they had thought he was out playing in the yard. When asked, he unashamedly informed them that he was simply carrying on with his "patriotic duties." His idea, it appears, had its genesis in a TV cartoon that featured a similar theme, where the main character took on the role of "flag police" during an episode. Inspired by this, and everyone's talk about 9/11 Tyler simply did what came natural, searching the Internet for information on proper "flag displaying," downloading that information, and appointing himself these "flag enforcing" responsibilities.

After a short lecture from his parents, Tyler was allowed to continue his mission. From this point forward, however, the "new rule" was that his parents would provide the "security and transportation" needed for him to properly continue carrying out his patriotic duties.

The Nurturing Toner

A couple of years ago, while part of my clinical duties still included consulting at various community nursing homes, I had the good fortune to learn about an exceptional individual with a very special gift.

One of the nursing home residents, 82-year-old Virginia, was known for walking around her wing and singing or "always humming" to herself. Since this was not considered to be a disruptive behavior, to herself or anyone else, the nursing home staff did not think much about it, and she was never referred for a consult or evaluation for this particular behavior. One particular afternoon, however, while I was conducting my rounds, the nursing administrator for that unit shared that, over the past couple of weeks, Virginia had been consistently going into a room occupied by a recently arrived resident who was finding it particularly difficult to acclimate to the nursing home environment. This resident, the nurse indicated, refused to leave her room or even open her curtains, preferring to remain bedridden day and night, refusing visits, crying, moaning, and talking loudly to herself to the point where her roommate had to be assigned to a different room.

Since Virginia had begun her visits with this resident, however, the new resident's troubling behaviors had been replaced by "quiet humming" and softly singing gospels. When asked, Virginia shared that her "humming" was in fact "toning," a practice that she had enjoyed as far back as she could remember, and added that singing was "the only sane thing in this crazy world." As we spoke, Virginia also revealed that when this new resident was admitted to the unit, she could tell that the latter was "in the wrong frequency" and so she began to make her visits, at which times they would engage in mutual toning. As Virginia sat beside the troubled resident, several times per day, she indicated, the toning would help her to "tune up…just as you would with an old instrument that needs tuning."

After our conversation I spent some time looking through Virginia's file which dated back more than 20 years. Her records revealed a long history of "diagnostic impressions" that included, among others, "schizophrenia, auditory and visual hallucinations, dementia, psychosis, schizoid personality, major depression, panic disorder" and a host of other clinical issues. Her "diagnostic list," was, as one would expect, echoed by an endless number of medications that had been tried to assist her with her daily functioning. A closer examination of her well-documented and thorough history, however, clearly revealed that this woman did not actually fit any of the clinical impressions cited throughout her records, but was clearly displaying many classical signs of Asperger's Syndrome.

All of these years, it suddenly came to light, Virginia's "atypical meanderings" throughout the halls of the nursing home while she sang and "hummed to herself" were her way of staying in tune. As we found, this was her own innate way of creating a sense of harmony for herself and those around her.

> In the state of "resonance" one can sense the surface, texture and density of material without looking at it with physical eyes or touching it with physical hands or tasting it with a physical tongue or tapping it to hear how it sounds...those who experience this condition can be "in resonance" with colors, sounds, objects, places, plants, animals, people... "In resonance" with people they can sense ("see," "hear," etc.) thoughts, emotions, pain, etc. of other people. (Bogdashina 2003, p.94)

> I might not always read faces or tones of voice correctly, but I can perceive people's emotions, through intuition. I'm sure the lot of you know what that is like. ("Wendy," quoted in Miller 2003, p.30)

No Drain for the Rain

During a consulting job in the Midwest a couple of years ago, I was called to assess a young man who had been recently arrested. Travis, a 32-year-old male, had been picked up by the local police after they had received several calls from drivers who had called in to report "a strange man, standing in the rain by the highway." Some of the reports even went as far as implying, or stating, that this man was "clearly up to something." After a brief introduction and review of the police report, I sat down with Travis, who seemed like a quiet, well-educated, and passive young man who displayed very little emotion and spoke in a flat, mechanistic type monotone.

Rather than offering a typical response to my basic question about his standing out in the rain and staring at traffic, reportedly for hours, Travis remained silent for a few moments. This lack of response, accompanied by his seemingly "staring off into space" while I spoke to him, and tried to elicit some sort of connection, felt awkward and could have easily been interpreted as "resistance," a silent "challenge," or an attempt to "be in control." His entire manner, however, was anything but "typical."

After his long silence, Travis embarked on an elaborate diatribe detailing the many flaws inherent along the road where he had been standing, each of which were creating unnecessary flooding that could very easily be remedied. He often drove along that road, he indicated, and during even slight rains the water would quickly back up, creating pockets of water that would cause even heavy vehicles to hydroplane as they drove through.

That morning he had taken it upon himself to observe the water collecting alongside of the road in an effort to figure out the "most efficient and cost effective way of designing a drainage system" that could remedy the problem. Asked if he was an engineer, Travis, still in his soft monotone, revealed that he was "just a store clerk working at Wal-Mart," but added that he had a "superior brain."

Travis was released after my evaluation revealed that his actions did not pose a danger to himself or others, and he was scheduled for a later, more comprehensive evaluation that would quickly confirm my working diagnosis of Asperger's Syndrome. Describing this situation to the police sergeant in the precinct, he quickly acknowledged the well-known drainage problem along that stretch of highway and even arranged for Travis to speak with an engineer about his ideas. Inspired by Travis's cogent idea for a drainage solution, and his selfless motivation to do his part for the community, the plan was proposed, accepted, and implemented within the next fiscal year.

> Many features of high-functioning autism (HFA)/Asperger's syndrome (ASP) enhance creativity. Certainly, the ability to focus intensely on a topic and to take endless pains to produce a creative work is a characteristic feature of this syndrome. People with HFA/ASP have an extraordinary capacity to focus on a topic for very long periods (days on end—without interruption even for meals). They do not give up when obstacles to their creativity are encountered. For this reason they can be termed workaholics and show a remarkable capacity for persistence. (Fitzgerald 2004, pp.2–3)

> I think spatially. An advantage of this is that I readily detect the structure or patterns of not just the objects but complex situations, which often helps solve problems that others with their more conventional thinking haven't. Spatial thinking has no limits, continually transforming and expanding to match any problem, contrasted with the limitations of words and categorical thinking. ("Ava," quoted in Miller 2003, pp.23–4)

The Rocking Navigators

Regardless of our destination, careful planning, and best intentions, our infamous "AS field trips" always seem to take a life and direction of their own. On one such trip to Washington, D.C., three of us "grown ups" escorted nine children (seven male, two female) all diagnosed with either Asperger's and/or nonverbal learning disability. Our mission during this journey was to visit, in due order and by democratic vote among the children, (a) the Library of Congress, (b) the National Cemetery where we could pay tribute to Helen Keller's and Annie Sullivan's graves, and (c) assorted Smithsonian buildings. Upon arriving at our first underground train station on our first day, all of us convened in front of one of the large, colorful underground subway maps that carefully and systematically outline the connections, directions, and locations that are joined through-out the subway system by a labyrinth of the cities well-planned public transport systems. As the three adults convened in front of this detailed underground map, trying to make sense of the "big picture" by putting together all of the "little lines and colors," we noticed three of the boys, all of whom are recognized as having AS, focused intensively on the map. Three of the boys, each of whom was passionately interested in "transport systems," were quietly standing behind us, rhythmically rocking back and forth, like three human pendulums, flailing their hands at the wrist in a synchronous fashion.

After a couple of minutes of conversation between the three adults, trying in earnest to come up with "the best plan," one of the three children kindly interrupted us by tapping me on the shoulder and saying, "Dr. O, we've got it, let's go." At that moment, before we had time to think, a train pulled up and its doors flew open, the three boys rapidly filed into the train, with the other children following them without hesitation, all the while admonishing us to "hurry up and get on!"

Boarding the "red line" at Takoma, for example, would take us to the Metro Center from where we could then take the "blue line" to the much awaited Smithsonian. The following day we would again take the "red line" to the Gallery stop where we would then switch to the "yellow line" on our way to the Pentagon. Later, we would take that same line back to the Gallery—which was how one would get to Chinatown by the way—and then re-board the "red line" on our way to the Woodley Park-Zoo later that afternoon...etc.

During the next three days, we no longer had to waste time checking the train maps, directions, or deciding on the quickest route to each of our intended locations. During that wild and crazy weekend getaway, we were safely in the hands of the navigationally correct "rocking navigators."

People constantly told us how gifted he was. He knew his shapes, colors, letters, and numbers by the time he was little more than a year old. He couldn't *say* them because he didn't really start talking until almost 18 months, but he could point to them. At age 2, he could give his grandparents detailed driving directions around town. He taught himself to read at age 2½. He knew all the states and capitals by age 4 and all the countries and U.S. presidents by age 6. (Klin, Volkmar and Sparrow 2000, p.444)

When we went to the store, the cleaner, or the park, I would insist on going the same way every single time. I would silently acknowledge landmarks as the route unwound whether they were the buildings and hills or the flowers and trees. I had memorized everything. (Prince-Hughes 2002, p.19)

The Screaming Circuit

When Hannah was only two years old, her parents were concerned that although she had already memorized the alphabet, could count and arrange the numbers one through one hundred, and could read simple text, she was still unable to use language for basic communication. Whenever she tried to communicate her needs rather than relying on speech, she would instead point to the desired object and utter unintelligible sounds. On the other hand her hearing was described as "highly sensitive." She would, for instance, often cover her ears and scream in certain situations such as whenever someone sang around her, rang the doorbell, or when a passing car would screech its wheels or hunk the horn.

One evening, Hannah walked up to a wall in the family den, faced a non-distinctive area, covered her ears and began to scream in a very high-pitch voice, almost like a siren. When her parents asked what was wrong, Hannah kept her left hand over her ear, pointed to a spot on the wall, and continued to utter her very high-pitched screams. Eventually Hannah's mother was able to calm her down by rocking her in her arms and taking her into the bedroom, where they both fell asleep while reading a favorite book.

On the following day, the same scenario occurred. Whenever Hannah would come into the den she would walk timidly up to that same wall, and, upon reaching the aforementioned spot, she would cover her ears, utter her siren-like sound, and stomp her feet. Visits to the pediatrician, audiologist, and a speech pathologist yielded no positive findings beyond very acute hearing. The parents' only recourse at that point was to simply not allow Hannah back into the den for some time.

A few days after Hannah's evaluation with the audiologist, and after her parents had put her to bed for the night, they retreated to the den to watch television. When they tried to turn on the den lights, nothing occurred. The lighting and the television in the room all seemed to have no power. After a few attempts at tripping the circuit breakers yielded no results, they gave up and retreated to their beds for the night. The following day Hannah's dad made an appointment with an electrician to check on the den's electrical system.

A couple of days later, after a thorough examination of the family den, the electrician turned to Hannah's parents and pointed to the exact spot in the wall that Hannah had been pointing to weeks earlier. "Right there," he said, "is your problem. You have a hot circuit back there due to some old

THE GIFTS OF ASPERGER'S SYNDROME

wiring that's probably corroded. You are lucky the whole wall hasn't caught on fire!"

Happily, Hannah began to quickly develop speech shortly after that event. Regardless, from that day forward her parents began to focus greater attention on her nonverbal communications and impressive sensory capacities. Realizing her keen hearing ability was truly a blessing, they also signed her up for singing and piano lessons. After two years of such lessons four-year-old Hannah is showing remarkable musical ability. As far as her hearing, her latest fixation is now climbing overtop of the family's upright piano and using a tuning wrench to adjust the keys whenever any of the notes begin to vary in pitch by the slightest degree.

> Albert used his auditory sensitivity to know when a train was due to arrive at the station, several minutes before his parents could hear it. He said, "I can always hear I, mommy and dad can't, it felt noisy in my ears and body." Another child had a special interest in buses. Before a vehicle was in sight, he could identify the make of the engine. However, he also perceived the unique sounds of the engine of each bus covering that part of the city. Thus, he could identify the number plate of the imminent but invisible bus. (Attwood 1998, pp.131–2)

> Hyperhearing (hearing "inaudible") is widely reported. Temple Grandin describes her hearing as having a sound amplifier set on maximum loudness, and she compares her ears with a microphone that picks up and amplifies sounds. They might be able to hear some frequencies that only animals normally hear. (Bogdashina 2003, p.54)

The Human Weight Scale

While in the checkout line during a recent trip to a local market, I noticed the young bagging clerk performing a number of subtle rituals that included lifting the grocery bag after placing a number of items inside, shaking it up and down, and then murmuring quietly.

As I slowly made my way to his side while he bagged my groceries, I did my best to remain inconspicuous as I watched what he did and listened more closely to his self-whispering. What I noticed was that he was carefully selecting and placing each item in the bag so as to construct a cozy interlocking arrangement in each bag. It was quite remarkable, for instance, how he could quickly survey the rapidly mounting assortment of cans, boxes, fruits, vegetables, and sundry other items, and choose which to select so as to fit snuggly into each bag. As he filled each bag up to his desired height, he would then gingerly pick up the bag with his thumb and forefinger, shake it lightly, and verbalize a weight, "Approximately 9.3 pounds," then carefully place the bag into the basket. The routine continued until all of the groceries were neatly in place, "Approximately 8.6 pounds...approximately 10.2 pounds."

"You're like a master at this, aren't you?" I asked.

"It's difficult to be certain," he replied, "but I can be sure up to a tenth of a pound."

The name tag on his uniform read, "Richard."

As soon as I got into my car, I quickly wrote on each bag the weight amounts that I had committed to memory as Richard read them out. The minute I got home I ran and grabbed a scale and weighed each bag.

Richard, it turned out, had been far too modest, as the weight he had called for each bag was correct to each tenth of a pound!

That very weekend I returned to the grocery store, excited to run into Richard and compliment him on his impressive weight-sensor mechanism. When I asked the checkout clerk about him, however, she informed me that he had been "dismissed." Richard, it turned out, had pointed out to the store manager that he was "bald," a fact which was hard to miss, and he was "let go."

A couple of weeks later, during a visit to a local school for an evaluation, I noticed Richard walking to class. I pulled a teacher aside and asked if she knew anything about him. "He's one of our boys with autism," she indicated, "but he's very high functioning."

Over the course of the project significantly more of the [high functioning autistic and Asperger's] group than the [non-autistic group] found work, job levels were higher; they were in work for a greater percentage of the time; and they received significantly higher wages. Thirteen different employers (mostly multinational companies) were involved during the course of the project and several were willing to take more than one employee because of their positive experience of employing someone with autism. (Mawhood and Howlin 1999, p.229)

The Auto Salesman

When I met seven-year-old Charlie, I greeted him by asking his name. His response? "What kind of car do you have?" His atypical reply to my typical question was so, well, atypical, that it took me a few seconds to actually remember what kind of car I actually drove, and had been driving over the previous six years. Having responded "Acura," he then asked about the specific model, type of wheels, engine size, and other details some of which I could answer, most of which I could not. After acquiring enough data to base an educated opinion, he first complimented me on having made "a wise purchase." He then pointed out some of the strong points and advantages of that particular model, all of which sounded strikingly similar to what one would read right off an advertising brochure.

Once he had politely shared the car's strengths, however, he then hastily switched to a detailed lecture about the inherent flaws that one may expect from that particular model, including—remarkably—a recall that had been announced by the manufacturer to correct a small mechanical problem.

After listening to Charlie's impressive assessment, I wondered what car in particular he would recommend. "Subaru Forester," he replied without hesitation, but offered no further comment.

"Why a Subaru Forester?" I asked.

Once again, Charlie went off on a lengthy, detailed dissertation including ride, agility, steering, crash-test protection, long-term predicted reliability, quality for the money, fuel economy, safety, owner satisfaction, cargo accessibility, standard all-wheel drive, acceptable acceleration with relation to fuel economy, and interior cabin comfort. He further recommended the optional automatic transmission, adding that I looked like someone who would "likely not be able to handle a clutch," as well as the turbo model upgrade. (Charlie was kind enough to repeat the above details while being tape recorded a few minutes later in my office, so that I could include them in this book.)

I was stunned. Throughout the rest of the day I could not help but re-evaluate my future car choices.

A couple of months later, Charlie and his dad came in for their weekly appointment, and the latter asked Charlie if he wanted to give me "the good news."

"Well, he probably already knows," Charlie said. "Now, how would he know Charlie?" his dad asked. "Because we've talked about this before," the boy responded. "Just in case, why don't you tell him?" the father answered back.

Looking around my office, as if examining it to make sure everything was where it was supposed to be, Charlie replied, "Yesterday evening we...well, actually my dad...bought the 2005 Subaru Forester 2.5XS L.L. Bean Edition for a *rock bottom* price, $270 *under* the sticker price, the deal was sealed at 6:42 p.m. It's a dazzling Cayenne Red Pearl color with astounding ride-ability. We were able to get him down on the price because of reported problems with the gated shifter, but that's just a minor concern."

That poor salesperson, I thought, he never had a chance.

Fixations might lead to careers, to accomplishments by some beyond the expectations of a generally unimaginative society. Who would have thought that Charles Darwin's boyhood fascination with bug-collecting would tell us about our oneness with all life, wherever it exists? (Ledgin 2002, p.18)

I am absolutely determined to be myself and I will not let anyone try to change me. I know my own mind and like to go my own way and do my own thing. For example, I would really hate it if anyone tried to make me into a non-AS kid... As well as gifts I also have challenges and it is the challenges which make me strong. (Hall 2001, pp.66–7)

The Two Karenas

Karena prides herself on the fact that she was named after her grand-mother, who, she adds, was of Scandinavian decent. When she was a little girl, Karena remembered, "Granny K"—as she is fondly recalled—used to read her granddaughter stories from Charles Henry Bennett's 1857 version of Aesop's Fables. Granny K, Karena recalled, could bring those old, sixth-century Greek fables to life. From those stories (the younger) Karena developed her love for birds, animals, and forests, all of which pointed her in her current study of ornithology. By the age of three, Granny K thought that her little namesake had memorized the entire book, when her little "magical girl," with hands barely large enough to grasp the large, engraved hardcover text, would hold it up and "act as if she could actually read it!" Little did grandma know that the younger Karena was, in fact, a hyperlexic child with Asperger's Syndrome who had not only memorized the book but could in fact read it.

Years later, when Karena was 16, her grandmother suffered a stroke that led to her being bedridden. Before long, the older Karena began to lose her desire to read, her favorite activity, and although only 58 years old at the time, began to feel that she no longer had a reason to live. Karena's parents, who by that time lived about two days' drive away from the grand-mother, decided to move back to their hometown in order to help care for the "older" woman.

Moved by her grandmother's deteriorating condition, Karena went on a personal mission. The book that Granny K read from, Karena recalled, was an old, hardcover edition that had been published by Macmillan and Company in 1883. All Karena had to do to recall every minute detail was close her eyes for a moment. In that breath, she indicates she could not only feel and smell the book—as well as her grandmother's perfume and body lotion—but could see it "as clearly as if I were holding it in my hands at this moment!" Closing her eyes and taking a breath as she regaled her story, one could almost see Karena literally reading the book's cover in her mind: "Some of Aesop's Fables with Modern Instances Shewn—spelled with an old English 'e'—Designs by Randolph Caldecott," the engrav-ings, she added, were by "J. D. Cooper."

A natural feature of child development is to have difficulty accurately re-calling events prior to the development of speech, yet some people with Asperger's Syndrome can vividly recall their infancy…The ability for the accurate recall of scenes can extend to remembering whole pages of a book. This eidetic or photographic memory can be extremely helpful in examinations." (Attwood 1998, p.116)

Karena then decided to turn her lifelong energy for pursuit of self-proclaimed "obsessions" into channeling her energies on finding a copy of that very book. Just a few weeks later the resourceful 16-year-old was able to locate an "almost mint" copy (considering the year of publication) and used her savings to purchase it for her grandmother.

As soon as the book arrived, Karena rushed to her grandmother's bedroom and asked her life's inspiration to guess what she was holding behind her back. After several tries the older Karena gave up, and her granddaughter asked her to "close her eyes and stretch out her hands." Having placed the relic in her grandmother's hands, the latter opened her eyes and thought she had been "transported back in time!" For the first time in months, Karena indicates, her grandmother smiled.

From that day forward, Karena and her family witnessed an incredible resurgence in her grandmother's overall health. She began to eat more regularly, exercise in her bed, and, before long, decided to get out of her bed with her family's assistance. Each night the two Karenas would snuggle in bed and take turns reading a few stories out of the musty old book. Shortly afterward, Grandma Karena finally agreed to undergo physical therapy and, within months, she was walking with the help of a cane.

Karena is in college now, finishing a degree in ornithology, but she's still Granny K's "magical little girl." Her grandmother, now in her "young 60s," spends her time taking long walks and writing a children's book that she hopes someday will be published.

> I seem to remember my own birth and elements of the few days following. Though this may sound like a fantastic claim, it is true. My mother was skeptical when I told her this as a small child, but when I described the rooms and events in detail, she had to concede that many points of my account matched her fuzzy memories. (Prince-Hughes 2002, p.15)

Nelson Kicks Bud

While discussing ideas for their annual fundraiser, the local sixth-graders decided to add a new "taste test" to their regular events that would feature a "Pepsi vs. Coke vs. RC" challenge. Their "ringer" was 11-year-old taste-king Nelson.

The contest, the authorities decided, would pit Nelson up against any community takers, kids or grown-ups, with all bids going toward a fund for upgrading the school's computer lab. A computer fanatic, Nelson needed no further motivation.

On the scheduled Saturday, the "taste challenge" began just as planned. Nelson, as was hoped, consistently identified the three soft drinks, while all challengers withered against his magnificent taste buds. After a while, one of the teachers decided it would be fun to up the ante, and asked Nelson if he'd be up for a "real challenge."

Having agreed, the teacher drove up to the local grocer and returned with a cache of soft drinks that would add the newly unveiled "Pepsi Edge," along with "Pepsi One, Pepsi Twist, Diet Pepsi, Pepsi Vanilla, and Wild Cherry Pepsi" to the lot. As for the Coke family, the enterprising teacher brought along "Lemon Coke, Diet Coke, Vanilla Coke, Cherry Coke, and Lime Coke." Nelson quickly sneered at this array, pronouncing the attempts to throw him "a sham." Thinking that the simple addition of "lemon or cherry flavors" would somehow trick his matchless taste buds was, in his opinion, insulting. In response, the teacher decided to further "sweeten the pot," and challenged the rapidly swelling spectators to increase their contributions in direct proportion to the young boy's unparalleled ability to distinguish between sugar and flavor substitutes.

Once again, the enterprising teacher made a quick trip to the grocer, now returning with Diet Rite, Mr. Pibb, Dr. Pepper, Diet Dr. Pepper, Red Fusion, as well as Hires and A&W root beers. So intrigued was the store's manager over this event, that he personally followed the teacher to the happening and pledged $100 if this "flavor prodigy" could, in fact, distinguish between all of their available cola-related drinks.

Nelson was unshaken by the unprecedented crowd. Nelson was given small samples of each of the above drinks, one after another correctly identifying each without hesitation. Only once, drinking Red Fusion, did he indicate that this was "something he had never tasted, but it was really good!" Considering this was a fairly rare product in relation to the others, an "exception was made." Nelson, however, refused to acknowledge the "exception" and insisted that he could not be held accountable for a product that he had never tasted before. He would not, therefore, "accept an exception," but he would accept "opposition" to including Red Fusion in the contest. The crowd wholeheartedly agreed with resounding applause.

By the end of the day, not only had Nelson's gustatory exhibition raised more money than all of the other events combined, but a local computer store that later read about the event in the town's newspaper pledged to donate a number of rebuilt, upgraded systems to the school.

Nelson's "sensory-enhanced buds" had made him a local celebrity and saved the day.

The Linguist

According to his aunt, who had been helping to raise him from the age of three, eight-year-old Clark had always shown a remarkable ability to pick up different forms of speech and language. Described as being able to "read before he could talk, and talk before he could walk," little Clark fitted the "Little Professor" moniker so often connected with AS.

It was just minutes after the conclusion of the 2004 school year and no sooner had the car door slammed shut than Clark reminded his uncle to "stop at the bookstore" so that they could pick up "the book and CD."

The CD, *Speak French with Michel Thomas,* was one that he had researched and identified as one which he would need to learn "proper pronunciation and the basic language." The book, his aunt indicates, was *Streetwise French,* by Isabelle Rodriguez. As he had been promised exactly five months, one week, and two days before, Clark's aunt and uncle had promised to take him to Paris at the end of the school year if certain conditions—such as improved grades, behaviors, and attitudes—were met. Confident that those conditions had been met, Clark wasted no time in switching his attention to picking up the book and CD he had so thoroughly researched and chosen as "the best choices" for learning to speak French "like a Parisian." Having learned the importance of "fitting in" and sounding "like a regular person" based on his past experiences with non-verbal struggles, Clark felt that this book, praised for its aim to teach "everyday slang and colloquialisms," would be ideal.

As his relatives prepared and packed for the trip, that evening Clark invested every free moment alternating between listening to the CD and reading the book. The next morning, as the family drove to the airport, Clark had now progressed to multitasking, listening to the CD while reading the book at the same time. So immersed was Clark in this "French acculturation" that as the family walked through airport security he responded to the security screener in French. The process continued throughout the transatlantic flight, with Clark rapidly leafing through the various book and CD chapters interchangeably in order to further hone his proficiency by practicing with anyone on the plane who would listen.

By the time that Clark and his relatives arrived in France he had begun refusing to speak English. From the moment that they stepped off the plane, and throughout the following week, Clark would serve as the group's official interpreter. Ranging from casual bantering and joking with the locals to asking for directions and ordering meals, young Clark had managed to acquire not only a functional use of the language, but also a respectable amount of conversational French in just a few days' time.

> Holidays at the beach would be a strange succession of lots of swims (the exact number and timing each day recorded in my diaries) and teaching myself French from the French books I took with me everywhere. ("Coa," quoted in Miller 2003, p.135)

> Reading French was not difficult at all. I therefore decided to focus on languages that involved only visual input. I took classes in Greek and Latin for two years and found them to be quite easy, as they focused on the translation of texts into English. I even briefly contemplated switching my major to Classics. I also excelled in areas of linguistics that emphasized visual input, such as syntax, which represented sentence structure in tree diagrams, and textual analysis. ("Susan," quoted in Prince-Hughes 2002, p.99)

The Anti-Smoking Vigilante

Regardless of whom you asked within their immediate or extended family, no one could remember exactly how early it was that Tanya had become obsessed with the dangers of smoking. Television movie? Video? Cartoon? Documentary? Advertisement? Commercial? Overheard conversation?

The source where this precocious nine-year-old "anti-smoking missionary" had first learned about the dangers of smoking had by now become a sort of familial folk legend. As a result, relatives, friends, family members, and neighbors who were regular smokers would wisely dispose of all tobacco products before entering Tanya's family home for fear of "being caught." So drastic was her vigilance that some adults even resorted to "running out for a quick errand" as a way of sneaking a quick smoke when she was around.

Having secured a series of pamphlets and brochures through the American Lung Association, Tanya kept a current, steady supply of anti-tobacco materials neatly catalogued in a small, plastic file cabinet in her room. Regardless of where the family ventured on afternoons, weekends, or holidays, she would not leave home without her "emergency supply." Once out and about, the young girl would not hesitate passing these out to total strangers at a mall, movie theater, restaurant, sidewalk, or any other place, supplementing her materials with a memorized lecture that continued even as the adult she accompanied whisked her away while in mid-sentence.

The lecture, as she kindly informed me, included research indicating that "Lung disease is the number three killer in America...is responsible for one in seven deaths...chronic lung disease includes asthma, emphysema and bronchitis...lung cancer is the number one killer of both men and women in the United States, and smoking is the number one cause of lung cancer...about 60 percent of people with lung cancer die within one year..."

Intriguingly, having learned from noticing people's reactions to her detailed data, Tanya always saved her punchline to the very end, accentuating the line, "and cigarettes cost a *lot* of money that you could spend on something useful!" as she was being dragged away from her hapless victims.

If there were ever any doubts that this young nine-year-old's knowledge and strong anti-tobacco attitude were not a serious commitment to her mission, her room was certainly a living, breathing monument to her convictions. In fact, a quick glance at the décor in Tanya's room would likely make the American Lung Association itself simultaneously envious and proud of the museum-like, anti-smoking exhibit on permanent display.

(The information that follows was provided in detail, along with photographs, by both Tanya and her mother.)

Even before entering, a large "no smoking please!" sign on her door alerts all who dare to tread. Rather than the usual pictures of movie stars and pop musicians, Tanya proudly displays three life-size, framed photographs of "healthy, diseased, and emphysema" damaged lungs. On an adjacent wall, visitors see a well-detailed, life-size poster of the human respiratory system. Atop her dresser sit two transparent plastic models of human lungs, one perfectly clear, the second coated with various shades of black and gray paint to simulate disease. Between those two lung models a large, green, broken glass ashtray sits as a symbol. A third wall features a large, heavily encrypted poster that lists every known disease from "A to Z" that has been connected to tobacco products.

The fourth wall displays a prized "Only You Can Prevent Forest Fires" vintage poster, featuring the famed Smokey the Bear, which a relative secured for her on eBay. Most creative, perhaps, is a register at the door featuring a challenge, composed by Tanya, that all who sign pledge "not to ever indulge in any tobacco product as long as they live" and to "take up the fight against smoking." To date she has collected 32 names.

Astute observers will notice the smiley face she had drawn on the circular fire alarm on the ceiling. Also adding charm to the otherwise morbid array of exhibits, was a "No Puffin" sign Tanya had secured; it featured a picture of a smoking puffin (the black-and-white seabird with a brightly colored bill) enclosed in a circle with a red line drawn across it, which she had purchased during a family trip to Alaska.

Reading material scattered throughout her room includes brochures on clean air standards, allergies, nicotine patches, asthma, indoor and outdoor pollutants, various "no smoking" buttons, tobacco fact sheets, a copy of the books *Smoking Stinks!* by Kim Gosselin, *Smoking, My Health,* by Alvin Silverstein, and *Jimmie Boogie Learns About Smoking,* by Tim Brenneman. Her bookcase, as could be predicted, features many other similar titles.

Andrew, seated in the grocery cart, spied three middle-aged women selecting sugared cereals with artificial colors. Before Andrew's mother knew what had happened, three startled women turned around to see the two-year-old standing up in the grocery cart, shaking his finger, and lecturing, "Put those back! Don't you realize that cereal is bad for you? It is mostly sugar, and contains artificial flavors and colors!" (Van Tassel-Baska 1998, p.107)

We can see in the autistic person, far more clearly than with any normal child, a predestination for a particular profession from earliest youth. A particular line of work often grows naturally out of their special abilities. (Asperger 1991, p.88)

Fast as Lightning

(This story was reported by a fourth grade teacher in Charleston, N.C.)

An interesting characteristic is that the child with Asperger's Syndrome may not conform to the traditional sequence of stages in acquiring scholastic abilities and may take some time to learn basic skills or acquire precocious or original abilities using an unconventional strategy. The child appears to have a different way of thinking and problem solving... They are just different, and for the child, they may be easier than the conventional alternative. (Attwood 1998, p.120)

Two fourth-grade boys were arguing over which superhero would win a foot race, Superman or The Flash. When Jacob, a fourth-grader enrolled in a class of children with AS, entered the conversation, one of the boys, aware of Jacob's passion for physics, asked him to clarify whether the speed of light was 186,000 miles per second or per hour.

"Depends on the media," Jacob responded.

"We're not talking about the media," responded the boy. "We're talking real life."

"The speed of light is the velocity of electromagnetic wave in a *vacuum*," Jacob replied. "Light travels slower or faster depending on the media, but different wavelengths travel at different speeds in the *same* media...when light changes media it changes speed...so, it depends on the media."

As Jacob walked away the two boys stood totally silent for a very long time. After a few moments of contemplation, they decided the race would be a tie.

On the Systemizing Quotient, males score higher than females, and people with autism score highest of all. On the Embedded Figures Task (EFT), a test of attention to detail, males score higher than females, and people with AS or HFA score even higher than males. The EFT is a measure of detailed local perception, a prerequisite for systemizing... On visual search tasks, males have better attention to detail than females do and people with autism or AS have even faster, more accurate visual search. (Baron-Cohen 2003, p.153)

Colors

During the first week of kindergarten, the teacher was introducing an exercise aimed at learning everyone's names, developing a sense of camaraderie, and, adding a creative twist, teaching the three primary colors and the seven colors of the spectrum. Using an overhead projector and color transparencies as visual aids, the teacher then requested that the small group of six-year-olds take turns sharing which of the seven colors of the spectrum was their personal favorite.

"Red…blue…yellow…green…" called out the children as each was asked. As it had over the previous five years that the young teacher had been using this particular exercise, everything was going smoothly as planned.

Then she called on Erin.

Erin, a small, thin redhead who had just turned six two weeks before the beginning of the school year was well known for her keen sensitivity and passion for colors.

After staring at the colors shining on the screen Erin gave the teacher her answer, "chartreuse."

"I'm sorry?" replied the teacher. "Which of *these* seven colors is your favorite?"

"Chartreuse," Erin replied without any change of voice modulation whatsoever.

The children snickered.

"Erin," said the teacher, "you need to choose one of these colors up here on the screen. Do you mean green?"

"That is not green," Erin stated quite decidedly. "That is chartreuse."

The snickering grew louder.

"The colors here," the teacher insisted, "are green…blue…red…yellow…orange…violet…and indigo…just like in the rainbow…*those* are the seven colors of the spectrum."

Looking up at the colors flashed on the screen, Erin thought about it for a few seconds and eventually replied, "Yes, you are correct, those are the colors of the rainbow, but the colors on that *screen* are chartreuse…cyan…firebrick 3…mustard…mandarin…orchid…and dark magenta, and my favorite color on that screen is chartreuse but my *actual* favorite color in the real world is none of those, my actual favorite color is viridianlight."

That weekend the teacher went to the art shop at the local mall and purchased a new set of color transparencies.

I like being different. I prefer having AS to being normal… I think that people with AS see things differently. I also think they see them more clearly. (Hall 2001, p.15)

The Symmetrist

By the age of two, Robbie's vocabulary was so limited that, for a while, it was a matter of grave concern for both of his parents. After all, Robbie's father, a draftsman, and his mother, an interior decorator, were both well-educated, professional people who prided themselves in developing their three children's natural assets even during prenatal stages. Well versed in the latest parenting strategies, they read books, attended seminars, surfed the web, and consulted specialists in order to continually enhance their knowledge of nurturing their children's talents and natural intelligence.

Although these techniques had proven impressive when applied to the two older siblings, Robbie's uneven display of strengths and deficits had presented a puzzle to his parents, their reliable and trusted family pediatrician, and a child psychologist whom they had consulted.

The perplexing mystery of Robbie, however, was quickly solved during an initial visit to a speech therapist. By the end of a speech and language consultation—his third—that was aimed at pinpointing his speech and language deficits, the astute SLP suggested that his "peaks and valleys" strongly suggested a diagnosis of Asperger's Syndrome.

Although limited, Robbie's vocabulary consisted of two words that made up a large part of his repertoire. Those two words were "wrong" and "right." Even before the age of two, his parents recall his pointing up at objects and repeating the word "Wrong, wrong, wrong, wrong, wrong!" over and over, sometimes unemotionally, other times with a slowly escalating passion that grew from a casual observation to screaming and furiously stomping his feet. For a while, neither his parents or anyone else had any idea why Robbie would seemingly stop on his tracks, point at something in a manner that appeared totally indiscriminate, and utter the word "Wrong!" for no apparent reason.

One evening, as Robbie's mom entered his room to tuck him in for the night, she looked around and noticed that everything in his bedroom was perfectly symmetrical. His toys, knick-knacks sitting atop his dresser, wall hangings, family pictures, everything within his limited reach appeared perfectly lined up and balanced. She opened his closet and noticed that, again, everything within his reach was also perfectly organized and in proportion to everything else. Moving to his dresser drawers she also noticed the same pattern—socks, underwear, shirts—everything was perfectly folded and orderly. Although she had noticed a tendency to keep things orderly and balanced in everything that Robbie did, the extent of this total environmental equilibrium had not struck her until now. Her son had an uncanny, natural ability for patterns and symmetry.

One night Robbie's mom decided to try an experiment. She called Robbie into his room and asked him to sit on the edge of his bed. She then walked over to his favorite picture and turned it on an angle. Immediately, Robbie pointed at the picture and began to cry "Wrong, wrong, wrong," becoming increasingly anxious with each repetition. As soon as she straightened the picture back to its original position he immediately said, "Right," sighed and relaxed. She then walked over to his top dresser drawer, ruffled his socks out of their alignment and watched him go into a tantrum, screaming "Wrong! Wrong! Wrong!" Quickly, she placed them back in order at which point he, again, sighed a sense of relief and said, "Right."

After putting Robbie to bed that night and sharing this "discovery" with Robbie's dad, they walked around their home and noticed that everything everywhere had a distinct sense of symmetry. Without realizing it, their natural inclination as a draftsman and interior designer had unconsciously created a living environment where everything was in perfect order. Robbie, it appeared, was the product of his ultra-symmetrical parents.

Over the next few days, everywhere his parents went they watched Robbie and noticed how he focused on everything in the environment. Whenever they passed something that was aligned or symmetrical he would point and exclaim, "Right," with a sense of peace and comfort. Whenever they passed something that was uneven or off balance he would tense up, point, and cry, "Wrong!" If it was something they could walk up to and align, such as a wall hanging or picture, they would straighten it, at which point he would sigh, and say, "Right."

Shortly after Robbie's mom's "aha!" moment, his vocabulary seemed to switch into overdrive and his functional language began to grow at an impressive rate. In spite of his increased vocabulary, however, the words "wrong" and "right" continued to be his favorites. From that point onward, whenever the family visited friends, relatives, and neighbors, they would have Robbie walk around their homes and point out all of the misalignments.

Upon closer examination, Robbie's parents determined that he was capable of noticing when things were out of line by as little as 1/16th of an inch, and that his ability stretched to every conceivable geometric shape (squares, circles, rectangles, triangles, trapezoids, and so on). Remarkably, they have more recently begun to realize that their prodigious son's innate ability is not limited to symmetrical proportions and alignments, but also fits in perfectly with the practice of Feng Shui, or the creation of balanced environments.

At seven, Robbie's skills continue to become increasingly more refined. Fortunately, thanks to his parents, Robbie's tact in sharing his observations of disproportion have also grown more refined. As such, the younger Robbie's "wrong/right" routine has developed into a much more sociably acceptable, "It seems to me that this shelf is out of line with the ceiling. Would you like for me to fix it for you?"

In spite of his remarkable skills, when asked what he would like to be when he grows up, Robbie still has his heart on one day becoming "a race car driver."

> At this point in my life it was the symmetry of the mechanical that I liked. Things were made to fit together in ways that always made sense, in never-failing patterns that had purpose. Machines were both reliable and aesthetic, the perfect blend of function and form. Looking back, I understand that I had a very developed aesthetic sense and was constantly framing the world around me with borders informed by purpose and balance. (Prince-Hughes 2002, p.25)

> To Liane Willey such visual elements as linear lines, symmetry, balance, straightness, perfect alignments, squares and triangles were appealing. (Bogdashina 2003, p.64)

The Spelling "Should Have Been" Champ

Stephen is a "spelling machine." He could read by the age of two and would drive people batty spelling out words all day long. As far as his parents can recall, "Whenever he saw a word, any word, he would somehow figure out its pronunciation, spell it out very distinctively, over and over again, many times. After that point, it was as if he had entered that particular word into his own personal data bank in his brain and that word would forever be logged in so that, from then on, he could just read it without much effort."

By the age of 11, Stephen had already won every spelling contest they had held at his school, his school district, local and regional events, and anywhere else where he could compete in his area. In fact, his reputation as a "master speller" had become so legendary that whenever other children, and their parents, saw him coming they would become visibly discouraged and sigh in frustration. Parents, sensing their children's look of utter futility in Stephen's presence, would bring out their best pep talks in futile attempts to lift their own children's spirits with variations of comments like, "He's just a kid like you…you have just as good a chance as he does," and, a perennial favorite, "Winning is not everything."

Having escalated to the brink of a national spelling competition, Stephen had just won his latest of many awards by successfully spelling the word, "zygapophysis." Adding fuel to his reputation, in this particular instance Stephen had gone one step beyond by correcting the reader's pronunciation of the word prior to giving the woman the correct spelling, and then, just for good measure, he added that the plural of the word ended in "ses." As was his norm, Stephen proceeded to do the above without any sense of haughtiness, superiority, or conceit, merely stating what, to him, was merely correct.

Having now qualified for the national competition Stephen picked up his trophy and rode home unimpressed with himself. After all, to him, this was just "something he did well" that required very little effort on his part. During the drive, as the proud parents drove Stephen to his favorite restaurant for their customary celebration, they proudly asked their son if he was excited about having qualified for the national competition.

"Yes," uttered Stephen. "Unfortunately, the date of that competition is in a direct collision course with Arlen's [his best friend] sleepover birthday party and, no, I cannot be persuaded."

Stephen's parents tried every tactic in their "parenting tool box" to convince their son that it was in his very best interest to miss out on his (only) friend's birthday party. Since the competition was several states away, there was no reasonable way that the family could coordinate their plans so that both events could be attended on the same day. On the other hand, while spelling came easily to Stephen, making and having friends did not. In fact, this sleepover party, for which he had been preparing himself for weeks, would mark the first time he had ever been invited to a friend's home for any occasion.

Stephen did not go to the national competition. In the end, his parents decided that, in the long run, it was more important that their son attend his friend's party than go to a competition that he did not care about, and that he, in actuality, had no guarantee of winning. Additionally, the national competition was open to children up to age 16, making 11-year-old Stephen a dark horse in the event. They also realized that another national competition was just a year away and, this time, they were careful to contract with their son that if he qualified again, the competition would take priority over anything else that would coincide with that event. Even a sleepover birthday party. Stephen agreed.

The morning after the sleepover Stephen returned home to a message from his English teacher who had watched the national competition. At the end of her general message to the family, she closed with the following question for Stephen: "The winning word, Stephen, was 'pococurante…'' Can you spell it?" Without hesitation, the confident young man, in mid-sentence of recounting the party's events to his parents, paused for just a split moment, and spelled out, "P-o-c-o-c-u-r-a-n-t-e… pococurante…and it is a noun…or an adjective," and with that, he seamlessly returned to the exciting adventures he had experienced with his friends.

Ironically, the word that could have given him the national title means "indifferent," or "nonchalant."

> Some autistic individuals are reported to be able to spell excellently thanks to their visual/photographic memory: as they read they quickly memorize the spellings of words; when they misspell a word they can refer to their mental catalogue of data to recall which spelling looks more accurate. (Bogdashina 2003, p.106)

Advanced vocabulary and spelling are two areas of common strength among children with AS and HFA. Norma is described as a sixth-grader who "could sound out and spell any word, even those at the college level. The school psychologist suggested to her teacher that asking Norma to tutor kids who didn't read very well might be a good way to increase her self-esteem. Norma greatly enjoyed her work as a peer tutor. It not only showcased her talents and helped her feel valued by her peers, but also allowed her to connect socially in a predictable, structured, and comfortable way." (Ozonoff *et al.* 2002, p.118)

Kaden: The Metric Machine

Although Kaden's general talent is in math, his "thing" is metric conversion.

Give this young sixth-grader any number, ask him to convert it to its metric equivalent, and he can do it without hesitation. Liquid, solid, speed, distance, regardless of the conversion, he can not only rapidly perform the calculations, but also cite the correct formula:

Centimeters to feet? "Multiply by .0328"

Kilometers to miles? "Multiply by .6214"

Grams to ounces? "Multiply by .0353"

Knots to kilometers per hour? "Multiply by 1.8532"

Liters to quarts? "Multiply by 1.0567"

Quarts to liters? "Multiply by .946"

Yards to meters? "Multiply by .9144"

Dry quarts to cubic inches? "Multiply by 67.2"

Liquid quarts to cubic inches? "Multiply by 57.75"

(Note: The above responses were obtained during an actual session.)

Perhaps most remarkable about Kaden's sensational ability is that he does not suffer from a lot of the daily living skills that typically accompany these types of savant, splinter abilities. Although he is a self-described "loner," who prefers to watch science fiction movies and assemble model airplanes rather than "hang out with other kids," Kaden is well behaved, does well in most other school subjects (maintains an overall "B" average), and shows just enough autistic-like symptoms to be labeled "on the edge of Asperger's."

> For almost three decades we were able to observe an autistic individual from boyhood to manhood... Even as a toddler, one could see in him a most unusual and spontaneous mathematical talent. Through persistent questioning of adults he acquired all the necessary knowledge from which he then worked independently... Not long after the start of his university studies, reading theoretical astronomy, he proved a mathematical error in Newton's work. (Asperger 1991, pp.88–9)

I also have some special gifts. These are things I can do like a much older kid, like reading and maths. And I was made a member of Mensa because of the high IQ result. I got quite a nice personal membership card with my name on it, but apart from that I can't say Mensa is very interesting for children. (Hall 2001, p.57)

Ace: The Inventor Atlas

Name just about any invention and 14-year-old Ace will most likely be able to tell you its reputed creator, architect, or discoverer. Although he has the ability to correctly name inventors about nine out of ten times on the average, like the rest of us, he has his favorites. These include automobiles, bar codes, anything to do with the Big Bang Theory, weapons, appliances, astronomy, motion pictures, musical instruments, television, and tape recorders. Whenever Ace does not know the answer to a question, he will say so, ask you if you know the answer, and, if you do not, he will look it up later. Whenever he is given the answer, or a piece of information that he is interested in but did not know, he will go into what seems like a short trance, and say, "Thank you." From then on that latest piece of data will be included in his "mental catalog."

Ace will also quickly, and without hesitation, correct anyone who is misinformed about the actual person behind certain historical discoveries or inventions. According to Ace, the telescope, for instance, was actually first developed in 1608 by Hans Lipershey of the Netherlands. Galileo's invention did not occur until a year later in 1609. The sewing machine was invented by Elias Howe in 1846, not Isaac Singer, and the original concept of the nuclear structure of the atom was actually set forth by Ernest Rutherford, in 1911, rather than Niels Bohr (1913) as, according to Ace, "most people foolishly believe."

Ace will also point out, quite excitedly, that the "infinity of the universe" was originally proposed by a monk named Giordano Bruno, in 1584; that Silly Putty was invented way back in 1944, and Monopoly in 1933; that René Panhard's 1891 model served as the prototype to our "modern" automobiles, not Henry Ford's like many people believe; and that holographs were invented by Dennis Gabor back in 1947.

"Most people," he indicates with a sense of excitement, "find that absolutely unbelievable and have to look it up! They think that holographs were invented, like, in the 1980s, but I set them straight."

> Some children with AS exhibit superior strengths or talents and therefore need to be appropriately challenged in the areas where they are gifted. Several inventions, discoveries, and works of art have been made by people with AS or those who manifest characteristics of AS. These scientists and artists were original thinkers with unique interests and abilities. (Moore 2002, p.43)

With understanding and support, we can develop and use our unique capabilities rather than be dismissed as disabled or made marginally functional by trying to fit neurotypical models. ("Ava," quoted in Miller 2003, p.57)

Griffin's Continuum

Griffin's sixth-grade social studies class project had been carefully designed by the teacher for the purpose of encouraging the students to learn more about their heritage. One of the children spoke about her roots in the Mediterranean, while another spoke of his family's proud Scandinavian ancestry. As some regaled the class with tales that bordered on the fantastic, like the child who spoke about "the family legend," which involved his ancestors being among the group who not only arrived on the Mayflower, but were the first to set ground on North American soil, others were a bit less sensationalistic.

Griffin, in the meantime, decided to raise his classmates' awareness of his family's lineage of "Asperger's Syndrome." It had not been that long, he told the class, since he had been diagnosed with AS. Shortly following this "great discovery," as his family phrased it, a number of the eccentricities that had been accorded to his grandfather and father before him, as well as a paternal aunt, had been thought to be decisively "Asperger-ish."

Griffin's take on his family's proud AS lineage, however, took a fascinating and fresh perspective as he decided to tackle the task of placing AS on a "normal" continuum rather than one that places AS on the "disordered" scale. "AS," he told the class, "is actually pretty orderly."

To illustrate his premise, Griffin requested that his classmates take their places in front of the class next to one another according to an arrangement he had been considering over the past several days. Without much introduction to his premise, he asked his classmates to stand next to each other, as physically closely as possible, as he called out their names in a pre-arranged order. Once everyone's names had been called, he asked the students to hold out their hands. As they held out their hands, he then asked them to look at the color, or skin tone, of their hands, then to look at the skin color of the hands of the students standing to their left and right.

Let's back up for a minute.

Since Griffin had the luxury of being in a class featuring students of diverse ethnic and racial groups, he had decided to take advantage of a unique observation that children in schools with a less diverse population may not have been able to appreciate. In effect, over the past week or so the young sixth-grader had been taking note of his classmates' skin tones, noticing that, from his perspective, they easily fell into a continuum. None of the students, he noticed, was actually "white" just like none of them was actually "black." None was really "brown" or truly "yellow." His idea, then, was to use this keen realization to demonstrate to his class that we are not as different as some would have us believe.

In order to make his point even more clearly, Griffin took a sheet of white paper and held it next to the student with the lightest skin in class. As he indicated, the little girl's skin was nowhere near "white." He then did the same for the darkest skinned person in class, holding a black colored folder against a dark-skinned boy's hand noting, once again, how this young boy's skin tone was a long way from the color "black." In fact, if you paid just a little bit of attention, as a whole, the class' skin tones were much, much closer together in color than the color "black" is to the color "white." When standing side by side, even a casual observer could easily see that the children's skin tones actually ranged from light beige, to dark brown, with many "beige to brown" shades in between, much like a multihued tapestry of overlapping color tones.

"When we talk about each other as 'black or white,'" Griffin related, "it puts us a whole world apart from each other, like we are two opposite sides of a two-color coin. But we're not at all, we're all much closer together than that. Also, one is not 'bad,' or 'good,' or worth more or less, it's all the same coin. Whichever way you flip it it's worth exactly the same.

"The same thing is true of kids with AS and those without," he added. "My father told me that people with AS are similar to people with ADHD, and dyslexia and other things that are learning disabilities but those people also have special talents, too, just like kids with AS, and everybody has something that makes them special or different. And like our skin colors make us different, but not so much, it's the same thing with being AS. We're all part of the same big earth-family."

Griffin earned an "A+" for his innovative and creative depiction of diversity spectrums. Additionally, however, his presentation so impressed the teacher that he had the opportunity to repeat it a few weeks later in front of the entire student body during the school's annual "Focus on Diversity" celebration.

> Diversity works well for me because my own differences from the norm are less visible in such a situation. ("Darius," a 38-year-old psychology student, quoted in Prince-Hughes 2002, p.19)

> If I could change one attitude in this world, I would change the attitude that autism is a matter of right or wrong. My child may think and function and process differently, but that does not make it wrong. My son is not

"broken": therefore, he does not need to be "fixed." Autism may be different, but different is not wrong. Diversity is cause for celebration, not for division. We may all learn more from someone who is different from us than from someone who is just like us... My son does think differently. Different is not wrong. (Huebner 2001, p.415)

The Family "Homonist"

As a toddler, Fonda quickly showed a remarkable grasp of language, being able to learn the proper pronunciations of even obscure words with uncanny precision. Soon afterward the meaning and spelling of these words followed. One of Fonda's problems at that early age, however, was that whenever she would learn the meaning, pronunciation, and spelling of a certain word, that meaning, pronunciation, and spelling would forever become cemented in her mind.

For years, Fonda remembers arguing feverishly about the meanings, pronunciations, and spellings of words that, although pronounced the same, were often spelled differently and had completely different meanings. It was not until the age of six, while in the first grade, that she learned that these words were called "homonyms." That was a long (well, relatively long) time ago and now, at the advanced age of 12, Fonda is not only her family's, but her school's—and very likely her state's—"homonym expert."

Among Fonda's favorite homonyms are the words "toon" (as in cartoon) and "tune" (as in a melody), "hair" (that grows on your head) and "hare" (a rabbit), and "moose" (a large elk) and "mousse" (a yummy desert). Having built up her homonym vocabulary to what most agree has now reached the point of saturation as far as the English language is concerned, Fonda's latest twist is combining them in phrases that she finds humorous (or is it "humerus?").

Some of the homonystic puns she displayed during our short meeting included, "Toxins (poisons) lead to tocsins (alarm)," "We (her and I) sure are a wee (small) group!" and "You haven't got a whit (significant amount) of wit (cleverness)!"

Fonda, who can carry on homonym-fueled conversations for sustained periods of time, hopes to someday become "the universe's first homonym stand-up comedian." However, she believes that her audience "will have to be made up of at least university students" as she feels that this type of humor would go "way over most people's heads."

> I am an intelligent, unsociable, but adaptable person. I would like to dispel any untrue rumors about me. I am not edible. I cannot fly. I cannot use telekinesis. My brain is not large enough to destroy the entire world when unfolded. I did not teach my long-haired guinea pig Chronos to eat everything on sight (that is the nature of the long-haired guinea pig). (Osbourne 2000, p.6)

Because they think in black and white terms, it is easy for them to learn phrases that fit into categories. For example, they may be taught phrases to be used for writing, those to be used when talking with friends, and those to be used when talking with adults. (Moore 2002, p.12)

Absolutely Quentin

Absolute pitch is the ability to identify or produce any given tone without the aid of a reference tone. Although it is often equated or used synonymously with perfect pitch, they are actually two different things. Having "perfect pitch" implies that a person is able to identify how close a sound is to being perfectly in tune. Some individuals with AS whose remarkable auditory memory extends into memory for pitch are also sometimes able to identify different pitches. Connecting the two, they can then sometimes develop absolute pitch.

Quentin, a nine-year-old child with AS, with no formal musical training has been able to label different notes played on various instruments as far back as his parents can remember.

"Any deviation from a precisely tuned instrument or performance," his mother attests, "will get him to cover his ears and scream, 'No! No!' as far back as when he first learned the meaning of the word. Before the age of two he walked over to his aunt who was playing a piano during a holiday get together, and kept taking her hands off the keyboard, screaming, 'No! No!'"

According to Quentin's mom, while most of the people in the room accused the infant of being "a spoiled brat who wanted all the attention," a musician friend who happened to be in the room mentioned that Quentin would only become upset whenever Jenny, his aunt, would strike certain "sour notes" which were—to him, and, apparently also to Quentin—obviously out of tune. It wasn't until this musician friend felt the need to come to the child's rescue that he too admitted that the "out of tune piano was driving him up the wall."

"At the age of four," Quentin's mother continued, "we took Quentin to a children's concert where one of his older cousins was performing. As soon as the first act began their number, a Mozart string concerto, Quentin began to scream, 'Help me! Help me!' as he covered his ears in apparent agony. It was immediately clear from the crowd's response that he was not alone in his appraisal of their 'talent.'"

A few months after that debacle, the mother added, Quentin was sitting in his room watching television when his father noticed that the sound happened to be a little louder than typically allowed by the family. Walking into his room, his dad noticed that the voices coming out of the room at high volume were not from the TV but rather from Quentin who was imitating the speech of the characters in the movie. That would have been unremarkable except for the fact that the movie he was watching was in Mandarin Chinese, and he seemed to be copying their inflections and speech patterns perfectly. His dad quickly grabbed a tape recorder that Quentin always keeps on top of his dresser, as he loves to record all sorts of sounds, and recorded him as he continued to ramble on in Mandarin. Later that week, the father took the tape over to Quentin's uncle, who is a professor at the local college. That afternoon the uncle called to say that he had played it to a gentleman in the languages department who identified Quentin's recording as "just about perfect Mandarin Chinese."

"Later that week," the mother related, "we took Quentin over to the college to meet the foreign languages professor, who, as it happened, specialized in Asian dialects. The professor played Quentin a few minutes of the tape his dad had made in his room a few nights before and then asked him if he could repeat it. Quentin immediately did so while the professor recorded him. Later, the professor indicated that Quentin had been able to repeat the phrasing on the tape with a variation of only about half a semitone between the two renditions. He added that, as far as he could tell, it certainly seemed that Quentin has absolute pitch."

Although the literature suggests that a fair number of persons with AS have absolute pitch, Quentin's auditory sensitivities seem to extend to the point where he can tell when a musical instrument, or performance, is out of tune to the point where the uncomplimentary sounds are physically painful to him. On the other hand, his parents report that throughout his development there has been no better, or more calming, elixir for their son than the sounds of well-played, in-tune music, regardless of the genre.

> He has a sensitive ear. I am a musician and have a very good ear but my husband seems to have a different kind of ear sensitivity. He can hear much higher pitches than I can… He pronounces the Chinese language with all of its tones very well. Many of my Chinese friends say his pronunciation is excellent. (Stephen Shore's wife, Yi Liu, describing her husband; Shore 2003, p.106)

> Some [persons with autism] have a very good auditory memory that enables them to repeat ("replay") long strings of things they have heard. Some can record musical pieces in their minds, then hum or play them flawlessly on an instrument later on. Some can "hear" conversations in their memory or even whole "sound situations." (Bogdashina 2003, p.106)

Edan's Adopt-a-Smile

Edan clearly remembers a day not that long ago when his parents, two older brothers, and younger sister were driving to their grandparents' home for the weekend. Looking out the window, as the rest of the family chatted and casually mentioned the beautiful scenery passing by, he realized that he was the only one in the family SUV who was noticing the disturbing amount of trash and debris that littered the sides of the roadway.

"Have you guys noticed all the trash?" Edan asked, but no one else in the car seemed to have noticed anything particularly striking. "Maybe it's the fact that neurotypicals sometimes don't notice little things," he offered as a possible explanation, "or maybe I just have a tendency to notice things that most people don't, or maybe it's both." In either case, once Edan pointed out the litter spreading throughout the sides of the roadway, the rest of his family became more aware of it.

"That's just the way it is," he recalls his dad saying. "People just don't care any more, the whole world is just becoming a big waste basket and there's nothing we can do about it."

As usual, Edan disagreed. As soon as he arrived home after the family's visit he went straight to the Internet and began to look for ways in which he could help to clean the environment. After just a few minutes Edan found an organization called "Adopt a Mile."

According to Edan, under the auspices of this program, a group or individual can "adopt" a two-mile stretch of land alongside certain roadways that they then become responsible for cleaning up at least four times per year. Since an adult must function as the authority in charge of these volunteers, this meant that 16-year-old Edan had to first seek out an adult sponsor. Within the next three days, Edan had already convinced two adults, a teacher, and a neighbor, as well as his two brothers and three students, to join together as a group for this purpose.

After many calls to the Department of Environmental Services, completion of documents, and coordinating of resources, transportation, timelines, home and school responsibilities, and other issues along the way, Edan was able to work through the deficits that he encounters as a person with Asperger's Syndrome, such as multitasking, organizing, time management, coordinating, and relationship building, in order to fulfill his goal.

A year later, Edan's original group is still going strong and together except for one member who has branched out. At a suggestion from Edan, that adult left Edan's group so that he could help sponsor a second group consisting of four boy and two girl "adopt-a-milers." Edan, as before, was instrumental in convincing this more recent group to join the organization and adopt their own two-mile stretch of highway. But Edan's persistence and love of the environment did not stop there. As soon as he convinced that second group to sign up, he has been an ongoing presence throughout the community, designing and handing out pamphlets made on his computer encouraging others at his school, church, and from surrounding businesses to volunteer their services.

As of this writing, Edan's efforts have resulted in a total of six active groups committed to cleaning up a total of 12 miles of roadways. Now, whenever Edan and his family drive along those same roads that he felt so badly about not that long ago, both they, and anyone else who cares to look, can clearly see the difference.

> Jasmine O'Neill describes an autistic person as the person who sees what is around him with extra-acute sight. (Bogdashina 2003, p.54)

> Many of us here clearly feel a connection with rocks, plants and animals. For me, this is not just an intellectual thing, it is something passionate and living, that I experience deeply in mind, emotions and body all at once (e.g., my response to a familiar tree). Bound with that is a sense of love, respect and responsibility for life, that is most simply and purely experienced in the world of nature, but which also extends to the complexities of human life and the wonders of the wider universe. ("Ava," quoted in Miller 2003, p.49)

Arif the All-Knowing

As an infant, Arif's father carved the word "knowledgeable" at the foot of his crib. When Arif grew too large for his baby crib, and upgraded to his own little bed, the father did the same at the foot of his bed. So, from the moment that Arif was first placed in that crib, the first word he saw when he awoke each morning, and last one he saw as he drifted off to sleep each night, was the word "knowledgeable."

"At first," Arif recounts, "I thought that 'knowledgeable' was the name for 'bed,' but then I just thought it was the company that made the beds, 'Knowledgeable.' One night, however, when Mom was tucking me in she asked if I knew why that word was carved there. As soon as she was able to stop laughing at my answer (that it was the bedmaker), she told me how 'Arif' is an Arabic name which means 'one who is knowledgeable.' Ever since that night I've always felt a lot of pressure, like I need to know everything there is, or at least try.

"When they had the elections for president in 2004," Arif recounts, "most of the kids in my class either didn't care, or didn't even know who was running, and I thought that was pretty irresponsible because by 14, which I was then, I thought we should care because it makes a big difference who the leader is of one's country. We had to do a special project for our social studies class so I asked if I could do a 'Mock the Vote,' which was like a parody on 'Rock the Vote.' But nobody wanted to do it with me so I decided to play both parts, President Bush and Senator Kerry, myself, then let the kids vote for whomever they preferred."

Arif went on to watch the three presidential debates, read the newspapers to learn about each candidate's views, and download information from the Internet. His main goal was to represent each candidate as objectively and fairly as possible. On "Mock the Vote" day, Arif set an entire platform up in the auditorium, and about half of the student body attended. The stage was set up with a podium, a stool at each side, microphone, two glasses of water by each stool, and two spot lights which would alternate from one stool to the other as Arif switched presidential roles. His social studies teacher functioned as the moderator and Arif, who wore a suit, alternated between stools answering questions in a one-man debate with himself. Each time he switched positions on the stage, to play either Kerry or Bush, he switched between blue and red ties. The "red" side stood for the Republican, or "red states," while the "blue" side of the tie symbolized the Democrat, or "blue" states. Later on his teacher went on to say that this creative flare alone would have earned Arif an "A" on his project.

But Arif, "the Knowledgeable," had much more up his sleeve than a silly, reversible double-colored tie. As he switched from incumbent president to senator, he adroitly adopted each candidate's mannerisms, speech patterns, and accents (Texan vs. New England), as well as their messages, superbly. By the end of the debate, Arif was, as he indicated, "exhausted but exalted!" He received a roaring standing ovation and, achieving his goal, gave everyone who attended a feel for the two candidates, as well as an introduction to their positions at the "red and blue" sides of the fence.

Arif had earned his "A," but, most importantly, he had lived up to his name.

> I've read that libraries are where immortality lies…. I don't want my thoughts to die with me… I want to have done something… I'm not interested in power, or piles of money. I want to leave something behind. I want to make a positive contribution—now that my life has meaning. Right now, I'm talking about things at the very core of my existence. (Temple Grandin as quoted in Sacks 1995, p.294)

> The high intelligence, technical abilities and impressive vocabularies of many Aspies have led to several nicknames for the disorder, including "Geek Syndrome," "Nerd Syndrome," and "Little Professor Syndrome." Noted autism/Asperger's expert, Dr. Tony Attwood further suggests the name, the "Frank Sinatra Syndrome," as the Aspie tendency to follow their own inclinations are reflected by the singer's popular song: "I Did it My Way." (Barrett 2003, p. HE1)

The Two Helenas

(The story below was submitted by Helena's mother and is reproduced verbatim at her request.)

I am writing about my little girl, Helena, whose most striking quality is her sensitivity. Helena is 12 years old and she was diagnosed with Asperger's Syndrome almost two years ago. She is in the seventh grade, which can be very difficult for many children, especially if they are special needs children such as herself. Although my understanding is that children with Asperger's Syndrome tend to be insensitive and unemotional, Helena is not like that at all. She is very sensitive but she just tends to show it in unusual ways. She becomes very upset when small children, especially babies, are crying or seem afraid and she tries to go to their rescue. Helena is also very sensitive about being teased, which she often is. The way she usually deals with hurtful comments is to draw the children who teased her a two-sided drawing illustrating how what they said hurt her feelings. These are done on a regular, 8 × 10 inch blank sheet of typing paper, which she folds in half so that she can include two drawings of herself, one on each side, so that they are both visible when the sheet is unfolded. On one side, she usually draws a smiling face, which she places above a positive statement or compliment, such as, "You look nice today!" On the opposite side of the folded sheet, she will draw herself with a sad face, above the hurtful comment. While some children have torn these sheets and thrown them away, most have surprisingly come back to her and apologized later. She will then reward them with a new sheet on which she will draw two smiling faces, with the apology underneath.

> My strengths give my building its character and enable it to stand alongside other buildings. (Lawson 2003, p.149)

> Also common is a highly developed awareness, not only of the sensory world as NTs experience it, but of an essence that lies behind phenomena, experienced as a "resonance" (rather than discrete sense impressions) which may include emotional and other undercurrents. ("Ava," quoted in Miller 2003, p.30)

Royal-Loyal Dalton

When Dalton was four years old, his mother just happened to walk into the living room when she saw Dalton's friend reaching up on his tiptoes to grab a crystal vase sitting atop a marble oval tear drop table. The vase toppled over and crashed into a thousand pieces. As she reprimanded the little boy for his trespass, Dalton, whom she had clearly seen sitting quite a distance away playing with a toy, immediately jumped up and stood between them, trying his hardest to shoulder the blame. Even at the tender age of four, little Dalton stood steadfastly by his friends.

According to Dalton's mother, about a decade later, when Dalton was in the ninth grade, a similar incident occurred. His friend at the time was not a very good student but Dalton was. This friend was the typical school goof-off, who spent a lot of time at the principal's office and getting into mischief. He was from a single-parent home and his mother was rarely around, so he used to spend a lot of time at Dalton's home. Since it was always hard for Dalton to make friends, and this boy tolerated Dalton's idiosyncrasies, Dalton's parents allowed their relationship to continue. While Dalton was a "high B, low A student," his friend was, at best, a "low C." One night his friend stayed over as the boys were working hard to finish a project for their class and they said they were going to go out for an ice cream. About an hour later Dalton's parents received a call from the police asking them to come by the station.

"When we arrived at the station," the mother recalls, "the police told us that the boys had stolen some knick-knacks from the store. The officer took his dad and I aside and informed us that the store owner had watched as Dalton's friend had taken the loot and hidden it under his jacket, even as Dalton tried his best to get his buddy to put it back on the shelf. Although he was not pressing charges against Dalton, the latter insisted that he had acted 'as a look out' for his friend, and helped him to 'plan the heist,' from the beginning."

Knowing Dalton, both the parents and store owner understood that he was merely being faithful to his friend. Thanks to Dalton's loyalty, charges were dropped and both boys were allowed to go with a simple warning.

Another, more recent story again demonstrates Dalton's loyalty.

Since graduating from college with a degree in business administration, Dalton had been working for an elderly gentleman in the latter's business. After Dalton had been working for this gentleman for about six or seven years a mall opened up right across the street from his mentor's business. Before long, the old customers stopped coming by, choosing to take their business to the more glamorous, modern facility across the road. Within months, the other three people who worked for Dalton's boss handed in their resignations and the business quickly plummeted. Dalton, however, stayed on for several months, helping his old mentor to keep the business afloat as long as possible. On two occasions, Dalton even turned down offers for more money, better benefits, improved working conditions, and a secure future at other sites.

"How could I run out on the man who gave me my first job?" he replied when asked to reconsider.

Eventually, the two men could no longer hold on and they had to admit defeat and abandon the business. Dalton's loyalty, however, did not end with "remaining with the captain in the sinking ship." In fact, the young man went as far as renting a truck, physically loading the office furniture, driving the truck back to the gentleman's home, and then helping him to unload all of the belongings into his garage.

Because of his insistence on staying at his old place of work, all of the good jobs in the area by that time were taken and it took Dalton a very long time to find another one. Still, to this day, he has never regretted having stayed.

"When Dalton was growing up he was said to be disabled," his mother avows, "but, actually, he is the most able person I've ever known."

We are good people to have as friends. We are loyal, truthful, honest and dependable. Sometimes people don't see our good qualities. This is their loss, not ours. (Lawson 2003, p.41)

Prospective employers should know that there are positive benefits to hiring someone with an ASD. Honesty, dependability, loyalty, and diligence are traits that can be found in abundance in the ASD population. (Sicile-Kira 2004, p.294)

Plainly Speaking Donald

(The following case story is a verbatim transcription as narrated by Donald.)

What makes me mad is people who do something, then say "I'm sorry," like that's going to fix things. I have news for you, it doesn't. If you break something and it can't be fixed, well, "I'm sorry" doesn't fix it, so they should just either say nothing, or say something more logical, like "I'll pay for it," because "I'm sorry" is not going to get you a new one.

Here is another one I don't like, and that's "unfortunately." That is a really idiotic word which they should just get it over with and take it out of the dictionary. If you go to a video store and they don't have the wide-screen version and they say "unfortunately we only have the full screen version," well, if I wanted the full-screen version I would not have asked for the wide-screen, I would have just brought it up to the counter and paid for it and been on my way. It has nothing to do with "fortune." "Fortune" would imply luck, or chance, or destiny, and none of those things have a thing to do with having the wide-screen version. You either do or you don't, so, "unfortunately" the person doing the ordering is just not doing his job. It has nothing to do with luck or destiny, or "un-luck" or "un-destiny." Here is a good twist on that, imagine you are very, very rich, and you wake up and your butler says to you, "Master, unfortunately your accountant ran off with your fortune, so you are bankrupt, and, by the way, I resign immediately, get your own breakfast! I'm sorry about that."

Other sayings I don't like are things like "See you later," "How you doing?" "How about that?" "Whatever," "It takes some nerve," "I wouldn't do that if I were you," "I can't put my finger on it," "Most people," "Bless you," like when you sneeze, and a million other things. None of them make any sense whatsoever, like, "I'll get back to you." What is that supposed to mean? Get back to me, when? How will you find me? How will I know that you are coming? Suppose I don't need you any more by then? This is why the world will be a much better place in the future when we are all programmed robots that just go on with our day without saying things that don't have any meaning. A robot will never say something as idiotic as "I'm sorry," or "unfortunately," because they just wouldn't care one way or the other.

(Donald is a 15-year-old sophomore in high school. His hobby is robotics and he plans to attend the Carnegie Mellon Robotics Institute in a couple of years.)

Joining an increasing number of adults with Asperger's Syndrome Gary Waleski, 36, asserts that he "was relieved" upon finding out that he had Asperger's Syndrome. According to Mr. Waleski, "it shed light on why I liked sewers and basement utilities when other children were into sports," and adds "it was like a weight had been lifted off my shoulders after all of these years." Supporting his belief that "understanding it helps others understand" Mr. Waleski speaks on behalf of AS through the Autism Society Ontario chapters, and the Geneva Centre for Autism with the goal of increasing public understanding of autism as not a "disability," but "a way of being." As he indicates, "it's like looking at the world sideways instead of up and down." (Miller 2003, p.1)

Rockin' Hoang

Whenever eight-year-old Hoang becomes stressed he rocks and hums. At first, it did not bother anyone in his extended family. In fact, when he was younger some even found it cute. But soon afterward the novelty had worn out its welcome. Hoang had grown out of his "cute stage," and the rocking and humming just made people feel uncomfortable.

"He needs medication!" some relatives would say. "He needs to see a therapist," came the call from some others. While some suggested harsh tactics, such as, "Whenever he does that, just whack him one!" others preferred the gentler extreme, "Whenever he does that, just give him a big hug." After about a year of trying everything from good neighborly advice to the latest medication however, Hoang just continued to rock and hum whenever he became stressed.

Another year of searching for the answer took Hoang and his parents on a trying journey that included various medications, stress management training, exercise programs, biofeedback, medication, many changes in diet, massage, and even chiropractic intervention, none of which brought any changes to his behaviors. Stress led to rocking and humming. At some point during all of these therapeutic visits, Hoang, who had been previously diagnosed with conditions ranging from autism to oppositionally defiant, was eventually, and correctly, diagnosed with Asperger's Syndrome.

One day, a friend of the family suggested to Hoang's mother that they try an Asian practitioner she knew who specialized in alternative medicine, folk remedies, and martial arts.

"We've tried all of that," the mother said. "None of it has worked."

"But this man is special," the woman told Hoang's mother. "He looks at the child's aura and his energy field, and this tells him exactly what the child needs."

Having reached her wits' end, Hoang's mother obliged, took the practitioner's name and number and made an appointment.

A couple of weeks later, Hoang and his parents all walked into the healer's office. The latter did not speak with the family, nor did he gather any information, but simply asked the family to come into a large, quiet room that was lit by many candles. He then asked Hoang's parents to sit on two chairs that stood against the wall, and asked Hoang to stand in the center of the room. The man quietly looked at Hoang for a few moments without speaking and then walked slowly around Hoang in a small circle as the boy stood quietly. The healer then asked Hoang to hold his arms to the side, loosely, and instructed him to take slow, deep breaths and exhale very slowly.

After a couple of minutes of watching the boy breathe in and out slowly, the healer took a position echoing Hoang's. Feet about shoulder wide, arms loosely outstretched to the sides, knees slightly bent and calmly said, "Now, you do this…"

At that moment, the man began to rock side to side and to hum. Hoang obliged. After a couple of minutes of rocking and humming in rhythmic harmony the man smiled and bowed to Hoang in ceremonial acknowledgement. He then looked at the boy and said, "Now, whenever you feel stressed that is what you will do, you will take a few deep breaths, and then rock…and hum."

The wise man then turned to Hoang's parents who sat staring in utter disbelief and said to them, "I have listened to this child's energy and when the child is stressed he should be allowed to rock, and hum, for this is what this child needs to do."

That was one year ago and, to this day, Hoang and his parents have not consulted anyone else about this issue.

"All along," the mother stated, "the boy knew exactly what to do, and he wouldn't let any of us change it."

Olga Bogdashina writes that it is unwise to stop these behaviors however irritating and meaningless they seem.

> It is in these circumstances of extreme stress that people with autism start humming, rocking, looking at turning objects, flapping hands and arms: "self stimulatory behaviours," involuntary strategies the child has learned to cope with difficult situations (hypersensitivity) or lack of stimulation (hyposensitivity). (Bogdashina 2003, p.16)

Swen and His "Theory of Mind" Theory

(What follows is a verbatim, unedited manuscript of taped comments made by Swen, a 14-year-old ninth-grader).

I looked up this "Theory of Mind"[1] thing and have thought about it extensively and I have reached a clear conclusion. It is a stupid theory. I think that having no Theory of Mind, actually, is an advantage. It is supposed to allow you to read other people. Well, people are not books, so you can't read them in the first place. If you fall for the Theory of Mind thing then you believe that you can figure people out, and that just cannot be done. Why? Because you are just then making inferences, that's all, just *inferences*, and that involves bouncing your own ideas of what you *think* the other person may be thinking into their head, as if you were that other person.

For instance, "I am Swen, talking to Vernice. If I were Vernice, what would I be thinking?" Well, I don't know, only Vernice does, and even she is usually not sure of what she is thinking about in the first place, so how could I? It would be a much better thing to just *ask* the person what they mean or what they are thinking. And if she doesn't want to tell you then it's better for her to just *tell* you that. So, girls who have Theory of Mind probably think I know what they are thinking, which is impossible 'cause nobody knows, most of the time they don't have any better idea than I do.

And this is why I don't have a girlfriend, because other people have Theory of Mind which is always getting in the way, or because they have it, then they use it to confuse people, or themselves, who knows. I'm not God.

So, to summarize, Theory of Mind is a stupid theory, or a theory about a stupid disadvantage which, if it went away, then maybe people would just start to *say what they mean*! It is just better to get the facts, say goodbye, and move on. That's all. And I would much rather meet an Aspie girl who would be my girlfriend and so we both would be lacking Theory of Mind,

---

1   The Theory of Mind hypothesis suggests that the impairments of people with PDD can be explained in terms of a failure to attribute mental states to oneself and to others. Without a theory of mind, people are unable to develop a normal understanding that other people have mental states, which in turn results in socially inadequate behaviour. (Ponnet *et al.*, 2004, p.250). Theory of Mind is also referred to as "mind-blindness," and, in general, refers to the ability to read what other people may be implying, or hinting at, when they, in fact, may be saying something relatively different.

but there don't seem to be any Aspie girls, just guys. So I guess I'm just going to have to make do.

I have to take into account that other people do not think in the same way that I do…having had to acquire this skill instead of being able to simply assume that I can use my own thoughts and thought processes as a model for those of other people is a huge advantage. It means that you are less likely to fall into the trap of believing that you know what other people are experiencing, simply because you (think you) know what your own experiences are. This is a great help when reading research articles and interacting with patients. ("Darius," a 38-year-old psychology student, quoted in Prince-Hughes 2002, p.39)

Moreover, it seems that NTs [neurotypical people] may have even more difficulty reading our AS minds, than we have reading theirs! And though a more-considered-less-automatic theory of mind may be disabling in social situations, it may be better for complex problem solving, and perhaps has other advantages over NT thinking. ("Ava," quoted in Miller 2003, p.25)

Chris and His Brown Paper Bag

(The following story was submitted by Chris's neighbor, friend, and employer.)

One morning, about six years ago, I noticed our neighbor's kid, Chris, was standing outside of his parent's yard washing their pick-up truck. His family had lived there for a few months and I would see Chris and his two younger sisters all the time, but never got much past the "How you doin', how are your folks?" type thing that one casually does sometimes with quiet neighbors. Chris was about 14 at the time and, although he was just about the nicest kid one could ever hope to meet, polite as can be, he didn't seem to have any friends. Anytime I saw him he was either working on something or doing something by himself.

The next morning I ran into Chris's father as he was pulling out the driveway in his freshly washed car and I took the opportunity to introduce myself. One thing led to another and I found out that Chris had a type of autism which was called Asperger's Syndrome. I had never heard about it before but, in my mind, it was about as unlike as autism as anything I had ever imagined. It turned out that although Chris very badly wanted to make friends, this was a very difficult thing to do for many kids with this condition. After a while of chatting with his dad Chris came out to ask his father a question and I seized the moment to compliment him on a job well done on his dad's car. As we chatted, Chris complimented me on the sign we had at the entrance of our driveway, which happened to be one we had done at our shop where we specialize in electronic message displays.

As luck would have it, Chris was an amateur designer who loved spending time in his room making signs for just about anything he could think of. His dad asked Chris to run in the house and bring out some of his work. Immediately, I was taken by the phenomenal detail and the creativity of his artwork. Although he had no formal training in graphic design or creative arts he obviously had a natural talent. With summer school break just around the corner I asked Chris if he would be interested in coming to work with me one day to see what we did at the shop. He was delighted and politely, but excitedly, accepted the invitation.

A few weeks later Chris spent the day with us at the shop, asking questions, observing, and even sharing his ideas on the color scheme for a design we were working on for a restaurant chain. Just as I had done a few weeks earlier, the workers immediately recognized the young man's keen eye for detail and color sensitivity. The other qualities that everyone kept noticing throughout the day, however, were his razor sharp attention and lack of shyness about speaking his mind when he liked or disliked something. Unlike many kids his age who may have leaned toward either trying to say the right thing, or trying to impress, Chris's feedback was refreshingly genuine and direct, but always presented with a unique blend of humor. Everyone loved him and we were all amazed that this great kid did not have any friends.

A couple of days later I asked Chris if he had any plans for the summer. When he said that he did not, I asked if he wanted to spend some time during the summer helping us out at the shop and maybe learning a thing or two about the business. He was delighted. The very next morning there he stood at the end of our driveway, wearing a white shirt and tie, and holding a brown paper lunch bag as he politely waited to ride in with me at 5:45 in the morning. For the rest of the summer, as Chris and I rode to work together I learned a lot about "Rush Hour" (a game about traffic jams and gridlock), brain teasers, mechanical puzzles, and Dungeons and Dragons, and he learned a lot about electronic display systems, engineering, and design.

That was six years ago. Since that day, Chris has proven to be one of the most dependable, ingenious workers any of us could have ever imagined. After working for us three summers in a row, and every weekend in between, Chris graduated from high school two years ago and is now attending the local college with a specialty in fiber optics and Goldleaf, although he also loves working with neon and has a special talent for sign carving. He still works for us on weekends, and each morning, without fail, there Chris stands at the end of our driveway, waiting for his ride while holding his brown paper bag.

Just a few months ago, in March, Chris accompanied myself and two of my colleagues to the International Sign Association's International Sign Expo in Las Vegas, Nevada, which opened his eyes up to a whole different world. Unlike most other 20-year-olds, however, what fascinated him most was the world of sights, lights and sounds that are inescapable throughout Las Vegas. To him, Vegas looked like "the ultimate interactive game!"

AS is a neurological difference that often *turns clinical* in a culture that doesn't value AS strengths. Much of our survival requires us not to become better functioning, but to better function according to the cultural hegemony of NTs, the neuro-typicals, who call the shots about what is valued in people. (Miller 2003, p.xix)

The positive side of AS is that we make good employees. In the workplace people with AS like structure and routine in employment, are punctual, can work alone, are meticulous, pay great attention to detail, take pride in their work, do not talk during work time and do not take days off, and can handle repetitive tasks. We tend to stay in positions for long periods of time and enjoy working with people who are motivated and do not mind isolation. ("Gary," a 27-year-old university graduate, quoted in Prince-Hughes 2002, p.7)

Sandy and Sandee, the Actresses

Twenty-nine-year-old twin sisters Sandy and Sandee took part in their first play at the age of four. Although the initial idea that jumps to mind of two cherubic-faced four-year-old twin sisters up on a theater stage may be of them playing two little angels, or a couple of adorning flowers, one must first keep in mind that both of these little girls have AS.

As such, during their first stage performance, the adorable, plump-faced twins climbed up on that large theater stage 25 years ago, and took their places a few feet from each other in order to enact their roles as…two stereo speakers!

The play, written by their 12-year-old brother, consisted of him "mouthing," or pretending to be reciting a self-penned poem—for which the audience held the text—into an microphone that was "connected" by wires leading to his two younger sisters who stood to his left and right sides. As he silently "mouthed" the words to the poem, the twins actually recited the verses, in harmonic unison, giving the appearance that they were his "stereo speakers."

Although that was 25 years ago, both women still remember the poem, and the moment, "as if it happened about three days ago."

During a relaxed conversation with the nearly legendary twins, they spoke eagerly about their fond childhood recollections, which included acting out movie and television scenes for their families from the age of about three onward, as well as their favorite routines, "role playing TV commercials."

"At about the age of five," Sandee relates, "we sort of started to ad lib our own lines into the commercial and that became even more fun." "At first," she continues, "the adults thought that we were just forgetting the lines, but soon they began to realize that we were actually being creative and I think it would sort of freak them out because we would just play off one another perfectly."

"We were always naturals at memorizing the lines," Sandy chimed in, "and even before we could speak we would usually respond to questions by using lines we had memorized from a television commercial or maybe a cartoon."

"And we would act out the character," added Sandee, "so, if the line came from a grouchy cartoon character the people whoever we were talking to would think we were being grouchy, and if it came from a character with a high, squeaky voice, we would just mimic that too, not only the words, but the voice inflections and everything. It must have been really hard to figure out where we were coming from!"

The ability to rapidly memorize scripts and role play a vast number of characters catapulted "The S Twins," as they call themselves, to rapid notoriety in their small, midwestern town where they spent a significant part of their childhood taking acting classes and participating in school and church plays on their way up the theatrical ladder to local and regional community theatre.

"It wasn't until we took drama classes that we began to understand how to socialize with people outside of our own family circle," Sandy states. "Our acting coach was a very sensitive, sweet man who understood that we were talented, but 'different,' and he knew that, socially, we were rather lost once we set foot off the stage."

Asked about some of the favorite roles they've played, or plays they have been in, the two listed far too many to include here. Among the highlights, however, were: "Sandy playing Hansel to Sandee's Gretel;" "The Time Machine," where Sandee played the current time character while Sandy played her "future twin;" "The Emperor's New Clothes," which both women feel is simply a story about being Asperger's; and a play based on the life of Annie Oakley, where the twins took turns playing the central role between scenes.

The theatre, Sandee remembers, has also always provided a safe refuge for the S Twins.

"If not for theatre we would have never been able to move to New York to attend school," Sandee indicates. "Regardless of where we go, as long as there is a theatre, with a stage, then we feel like we are home. There is a certain smell and feel, not only to theaters, but also to actors, that is very unique and very comfortable."

Sandy and Sandee are both successful professional actresses now and, although they strongly prefer dramatic theatre, they have also played numerous minor roles, both individually and together, in television, movies, and, yes, TV commercials. Together with their older brother, who is a scriptwriter, they are currently working on a manuscript about, what else, twin sisters who move to the big city and make it big!

I never mention social skills or Asperger's Syndrome. Sometimes my students do, but we don't dwell on it. In my opinion, these kids could use a break from their autism diagnosis. The only time I mention it is to tell them that because of their diagnosis, they have a predisposition to becoming talented actors. This is why, I tell them, I have hand picked them to be in my advanced acting class. And, as any actor, they will be working hard. (Davies 2004, p. xix)

I have taught many levels of acting, from beginner to advanced and I can honestly say that each class of Asperger's students has contained more charisma and raw talent than many of my collegiate or G.A.T.E. level classes. (Davies 2004, p.4)

Nathan, the Computer Geek

Nathan is a computer geek. It is his badge of honor; he distinguishes himself by it. His favorite movie of all time is *Napoleon Dynamite* and so enamored is he by the main character that he even had his hair permed in order to emulate him.

> I *love* my computers. ("Kalen," quoted in Miller 2003, p.45)

Six months ago Nathan's parents were extremely worried about their 16-year-old son, who was diagnosed at the age of eight with Asperger's Syndrome, because, according to them, "no one would have anything to do with him." At that time, Nathan's family had just relocated to a different state, and the young man, who had been attending a school that afforded him the luxury of a small class and special services, suddenly found himself in a new state, town, school and classroom with over 40 virtual strangers. In this new school, Nathan had no acquaintances, was disoriented, anxious, and he was becoming increasingly depressed.

Nathan's situation, however, changed during one fateful afternoon. The student body had assembled at the school auditorium to watch a performance by a local hip-hop group that depended on their computers for all of their sounds and light effects. About a minute into their performance, just as the students' juices had begun to flow in the audience, the main computer "crashed" and the performers were left standing in the center of the stage looking completely helpless. As the students waited, some more patiently and politely than others, the school's "tech person" came by to assess the problem. After a few minutes, he informed the performers that, unfortunately, there was nothing he could do. The hard drive was "gone," and "all of the files would be lost."

Nathan, who was sitting in the first row, fully focused and attentive as usual, overheard the drastic news. Undaunted, as the rest of the student body sat at the brink of anarchy, he walked on the stage and asked if he could take a look at the system. Within minutes, the computer was up and running and the files had been recovered. Asked why he felt the school's hired specialist had been unable to find a solution, especially when he had done so, so rapidly, Nathan shrugged his shoulders and offered, "he's probably just too old." (The school's computer tech, we later learned, is 26 years old.)

Most AS kids relate better to computers than people so working on a laptop or word processor will enable them to work better and faster. (Jackson
2002, p.123)

Thanks to Nathan, the show went on as promised. The feat so impressed
Nathan's peers that his legend spread like wildfire. So magnanimous had
been Nathan's great feat that it even became the lead story in the school's
weekly newspaper, where he was featured posing with the performers.

Six months later Nathan can't find enough time in his schedule to fit
people in who are in desperate demand for his services. Suddenly, he is the
school's "computer expert." Weeknights, Nathan limits his computer consulting services time to "two hours maximum" for which he charges $75
per hour (his initial fee started at $25 per hour but quickly escalated), with
most of his work coming from computer-challenged adults from his
church, parents of school peers, and people from all around his community.
He limits his Saturday work hours to six, at the request of his parents, and is
putting his money away for college.

Having found his niche, Nathan's popularity, and his unique sense of
humor, has endeared him to many of his schoolmates who are now
inviting him on a regular basis to parties, outings, and other peer-related
functions. Being so highly in demand, Nathan confesses—in his straightforward, unpretentious manner—he "tries to make an appearance" at these
functions, "whenever I can fit them into my schedule."

Indeed, by adolescence, a few of the gifted children with AS in this study
were willing to share information and to instruct in a topic or skill area in
which they had expertise, such as chess playing, computers, or math,
without any thought of getting payment for it. They also were willing to
listen to advice, particularly information-based advice. If they were in error, and it was pointed out, they were usually willing to change their data
to match the new facts in evidence. (Lovecky 2004, p.364–5)

Portrait by Helen

When Helen was eight years old she painted a portrait and taped it up on the refrigerator door. At the bottom, and to the right, she signed it with her usual, "Portrait by Helen." When her mother saw it she thought it was lovely, as usual. Helen had been painting portraits of everyone she knew for years now, and everyone knew she was an exceptional talent.

But this drawing was different.

When Helen's mom asked her who the young woman was in the picture, her daughter told her it was herself, at the age of 18. Helen explained that she wanted to see what she would look like "ten years from now," and so decided to, well, just "look ahead and draw it." Her mother was speechless. Not only did this have no precedent as far as the mother could figure out but, according to the mother's own artistic judgment, with a little imagination, this "future projected" self-portrait was eerily accurate.

After showing the portrait to Helen's father, who was just as awestruck as the mother had been, they asked Helen if she could try her hand at drawing herself at a later age, say, 26. Helen happily obliged and the result was at least as stunning as the first. They then asked the little girl if she could try sketching them, ten years from now. Once she had completed their future portraits, the parents asked Helen to do the same with the images of her two older sisters, who were 12 and 15 years old at the time. The results were consistently dramatic.

So dramatic, in fact, that Helen's parents decided to send pictures of them, Helen, and her two sisters to a studio that specialized in taking current photos and manipulating them via computer to look as each person might at various developmental stages in the future. Again, the outcome was uncanny as the details in the future-projected portraits resembled the characteristics in Helen's drawings in every notable way.

Not stopping there, Helen's father, who was a physician, took Helen's portraits, a set of family photographs, and the computer company's future-projection portraits to a friend who was a well-known cosmetic surgeon in their town. The surgeon, who prides himself in constantly maximizing his expertise on human facial anatomy by taking art, sculpting, and other related classes was astounded. Not only was her artwork exceptional, but her ability to extrapolate into the future was, as he termed it, "a little creepy."

Although Helen's parents have no idea how long this unique, inherent ability, or set of abilities, will last, they are certain that it "has something to do with her 'being Asperger's.'" Likewise, regardless of where these talents may, or may not, take their little girl from this point forward, both parents are ready to support and encourage her gifts in whatever direction they may lead her.

Since I was able to hold a pencil, I have been drawing. I am a visual thinker, which is, of course, not unusual for those on the autistic spectrum. I tend to record images and store them somewhere in the recesses of my brain's memory banks, to be later drawn in great detail. Since my drawings were easily understood by grownups, they made a lot of fuss over them. They saw a lot of things that caused them to react in astonishment. They called me unusually talented, and even a kind of prodigy. ("Wendy," quoted in Miller 2003, p.123)

Temple [Grandin] has always been a powerful visualizer… She had no sense that she could draw, make blueprints, until she was twenty-eight, when she met a draftsman and watched him drawing plans. "I saw how he did it," she told me. "I went and got exactly the same instruments and pencils as he used…and then I started pretending I was him. The drawing did itself, and when it was all done I couldn't believe I'd done it. I didn't have to learn how to draw or design, I pretended I was David—I appropriated him, drawing and all." (Sacks 1995, p.266)

CHAPTER 3

*T*he World of Gainful Employment

The goal of this section is to illustrate how "Aspies" can be, and often are, fully functioning, productive, and happy individuals who live regular lives while making invaluable contributions to society. As can be seen throughout this section, the talents, gifts, hobbies, and natural abilities presented in the earlier chapters can at times lay the groundwork for dynamic career paths, or directly contribute to their vocational pursuits, achievements, and aspirations.

> Intellectually able + AS + Area of passionate interest = Academic success (Harpur *et al.* 2003, p.242)

> Able autistic individuals can rise to eminent positions and perform with such outstanding success that one may even conclude that only such people are capable of certain achievements. It is as if they had compensatory abilities to counter-balance their deficiencies. Their unswerving determination and penetrating intellectual powers, part of their spontaneous and original mental activity, their narrowness and single-mindedness, as manifested by special interests, can be immensely valuable and can lead to outstanding achievements in their chosen areas. (Asperger, 1991, p.88)

Findings from a research article published in the journal *Educational Psychology in Practice* (Connor 2000) provide feedback from a number of secondary-school-level students with Asperger's Syndrome about what they wanted to do after finishing school. Popular choices were to work with computers (or designing computer games); to become a designer (aircraft, military vehicles, gardens); and to go to college. Asked "what helps them to learn best," the students responded: working in small groups—especially with a choice of activity; working on their own—especially with a computer; and working with one or two others—because they did not like talking in front of a whole group. This is an important point because, as Liane Holliday Willey notes: "Adults with Asperger who consider themselves to be happy and well adjusted frequently come from the backgrounds where their individuality was applauded and their abilities were supported" (Willey 2003, p.205).

> When it comes to careers, people with ADHD and autistic spectrum disorders possess a creativity that is unmatched in the common worker. If a problem needs solving and it takes out-of-the box thinking to solve it, you can be sure that the employee with ADHD or an autistic spectrum disorder will be among the first to come up with a solution. (Kennedy 2002, pp.102–3)

According to Yvona Fast (2004, pp.213–7), when applied in the workplace, typical characteristics of persons with Asperger's Syndrome can be extremely beneficial and considered marketable strengths. In her book *Employment for Individuals with Asperger's Syndrome or Non-Verbal Learning Disabilities*, she notes many typical AS characteristics that stand individuals in good stead in the workplace. These include intelligence, attention to detail, enthusiasm for a topic of interest, perseverance, thoroughness, having an excellent memory, articulateness, honesty and a straightforward attitude, being a hard worker, friendliness and helpfulness, and adherence to rules.

Yvona Fast offers the following advice for concerned persons with AS who fear that their deficits, or particular characteristics, may tend to leave a poor impression:

> Mention the positive traits—your laser-like concentration and ability to stick with a project, or your wordsmith abilities: for example: "I have a condition which makes it difficult to deal with interruptions and multi-tasking. However, it also gives me great powers of concentration, and I'm able to work on a project or problem for a very long time." (Fast 2004, p.251)

Calix: Graphic Artist

Calix, who is 37 years old, has what many—be it someone with AS or not—would consider an ideal, if not perfect, job. Feeling he "didn't really fit in anywhere" between the years of middle school and high school, he found himself becoming more and more of a loner. Because of that, he would often spend a lot of energy and time trying to figure out "all the good hiding places" at his school so that he could be left alone and work on his personal interests. On one particular afternoon, during his lunch time, he wandered into the school's print shop. There, Calix, a ninth-grader at the time, met another young man, a senior, whom he describes as "the twin brother I never knew I had."

In many ways, Calix's older colleague reminded him of himself. He was not particularly social, was not interested in sports, and did not care much for typical extracurricular activities. Because of that, this young man had, during his sophomore year, founded the school's small newspaper and single-handedly started his own school-funded printing press. Being a voracious reader and "amateur science fiction cartoonist," Calix felt an instant kinship with the older boy who shared many similar interests.

> When I close my eyes, I can play it back like a three-dimensional tape, replete with the smells, the sensations, and my feelings about it. I have always had this photographic or eidetic memory, and all of my many recollections of the past have a quality that makes them seem almost more real than the present. They allow me to tell the story of my life. (Prince-Hughes 2002, p.16)

From that day onward, Calix began to spend all of his free time at the school's printing press, where he also began an informal apprenticeship under the tutelage of his friend who would be graduating by year's end. Little did Calix know at the time that the fateful encounter during a lonely afternoon would provide a perfect haven throughout his school years, much less a career blueprint for his life.

After graduation, Calix went to college where he majored in illustration and graphic design. With his previous experience in printing, multimedia, and online work, the transition to college was made rather smoothly and successfully. In college, he gained further training and experience, branching out into web and game design and animation. Being in an environment where he was around a number of "kindred spirits," Calix was more comfortable now than he had ever been in high school. Further,

THE WORLD OF GAINFUL EMPLOYMENT

the common background of those pursuing similar degrees made for less stressful social encounters as well an increased ability for engaging in teamwork.

Although Calix describes himself as a "digital" or "commercial" artist, he indicates that he is quite comfortable working in multimedia projects. As an animator, he prefers Flash and Gift Builder, and when engaged in graphic design he prefers QuarkXPress. For 3D illustration Calix states he feels most comfortable with Lightwave, Maya, D Studio, and Form Z. Overall, he feels proficient at "just about anything new that comes out," and adds that he often also uses Photoshop, Freehand, and Illustrator, all of which makes him incredibly marketable in his field.

Among the many things that Calix loves about his work is the fact that he gets to be creative and "work at his own pace, sometimes from home, other times from the office. If I feel like not coming in until noon, and working until 2:00 a.m. in the morning, then that's what I do. Other times I will just be in the office for days, and will completely lose track of time. I might think it's still Monday morning, and before I realize it, it's Wednesday night!"

Calix, who describes himself as a "visual thinker," is currently becoming more proficient at developing video games. His dream is to create "the definitive game, one that goes around forever, and never ends, because you never want it to."

Jacqui: Archeologist

Jacqui, a 27-year-old field archeologist with an anthropology M.A. degree in social and behavioral sciences, has been stationed at an excavation and exploration site in northern Africa for the past two and one-half years. Her specialties include Near Eastern, Egyptian, and Mediterranean civilizations. In college, her favorite subjects were cultural anthropology, historical archeology, material culture and folklore, theology, social inequality, and ancient civilizations. Her favorite time periods were the Predynastic (5500–3100 BC) and the First Persian (525–404 BC), and her favorite pharaoh was Hatshepsut, the female pharaoh.

She recalls first reading about Hatshepsut in the eighth grade and becoming completely enamored with the stories, the time period, and even the sound of the name.

"Hatshepsut (1473–1458 BC) was the daughter of Thutmose I, and Queen Ahmose Nefertari," Jacqui told me. "I always thought it was awesome that she actually had herself crowned 'king,' and is always portrayed wearing a royal fake beard!"

Jacqui feels that she is a visual-solitary thinker. "I had never thought of it in those terms, but I am very introspective and independent. I like my quiet time and independence and would rather work for myself, but in this field of work that would be very difficult to do. As far as a 'thinking-style,' however, I would certainly describe myself as visual. When I come up against a road block I close my eyes and try to figure out the best way out, or around it. I'm not one to back off or turn and run the other way, never have been. Obviously, I like being in remote, solitary places, so having a good, vivid imagination is a great attribute in my case."

Jacqui's interest in "amateur" archeology, as she refers to it, began when she was about five years old, instinctively digging for whatever she could find in her grandmother's back yard in Arizona. "When I was a little girl, kids used to tease me and call me 'dinosaur girl,' because I used to bury toy dinosaur models as deep as I could, all over grandma's property, draw a map of where they were, then come back a few days later and dig them out. I would make all sorts of elaborate markings on the map, my own hiero-glyphics, to make sure that if anything happened to me no one would be able to find them—unless they were really sharp. I thought that if something were to happen to me those buried dinosaurs would be my legacy. I would also make up languages that I would use whenever I talked with the dinosaurs, and I'd pretend I was from the future unearthing these precious relics."

In other kids' eyes, Jacqui was "pretty weird." "I was never one to play with dolls, at least not in the typical way. As a matter of fact, whenever I got a doll for some reason or another—which was rare because I only wanted dinosaurs—I would bury them as well. Embalm them, wrap them up like mummies and bury them as deep as I could. My grandfather, whom I now realize was a classic Aspie, was the only one who understood. He would help me figure out different ways of making embalming fluid, and we would go in his workshop and make tiny little wooden caskets for them."

Jacqui feels that her type of work is tailor-made for Aspies like herself. She feels that her visual-spatial abilities, "laser-type" focusing, and patience for topics she likes (such as excavation of Egyptian artifacts) are unrivaled. She feels that her "Aspie mind" was essential in helping her focus and excel at school, as well as in her work, while keeping distractions out.

"While other students were out partying and switching majors, I had a single-minded attitude about what I wanted to do, and where I was heading. I also had more practical goals in mind than a lot of my peers. While some of them would sit around talking about the next great find of the twentieth and twenty-first centuries, my mind set was on finding a job doing field work and traveling around northern Africa and the Middle East."

Rather than merely collecting and arranging things, some gifted children with AS, especially those with very high IQ scores, are more likely to classify material, and to integrate it with other areas of knowledge. Stuart, a gifted 13-year-old boy with AS…began to think about how the changing of maps through the ages represented major historical events. He began to study these events and to draw his own ideas about how the maps had looked at different points in history. This led to theorizing about how different forces change maps over time. (Lovecky 2004, p.142)

Naresh: Engineer

Twenty-nine-year-old Naresh, an electrical engineer, feels that the general notion that the various fields of engineering are particularly attractive to persons with Asperger's Syndrome is fairly accurate. "In general," he indicates, "I think that our minds are wired in ways that are somewhat conducive to working with scientific knowledge in order to solve technical problems and developing products and services. I've noticed that not only in electrical engineering, but in areas such as physics, math, materials sciences, and mechanics one is likely to find a lot of Aspies, although regular people, outside of the spectrum, would have no idea who we are.

"Personally, I am involved in research, testing, design, and development of electronic systems. My specialty is electric motors but I also enjoy working with computer hardware and writing specifications. Currently, my research involves dealing with energy generation through wind, geothermal, fuel cell, turbine, hydro, and solar methods. Things I am not interested in, and that I would not be good at, include department or project management, supervision, or any type of administrative work."

Naresh describes himself as a visual-mathematical thinker who loves any and all number-type challenges. "I like to work things out in sequential, systematic ways, actually coming up with twists and shortcuts to accepted or traditional strategies. I always felt I could have made a great detective because I have a knack for picking up on logical flaws and slip-ups, so I think I would be able to logically figure out some of the devious ways of criminal minds."

> During my career, I have met many brilliant visual thinkers working in the maintenance departments of meat plants. Some of these people are great designers and invent all kinds of innovative equipment, but they were disillusioned and frustrated at school. Our educational system weeds these people out of the system instead of turning them into world-class scientists. (Grandin 1995, p.186)

Although the common perception is that persons with AS have a difficult time getting through the initial job interview, this was not an issue for Naresh. According to him, after a lot of failed "mock interviews" during his final year in college, he decided to just apply for a position and "be himself." When he arrived at the work site and met his interviewer, and future boss, he realized that he was face to face with "someone who understood Aspies. Although not an Aspie himself, it was obvious that this person recognized one of us when he met us, and knew that we tend to be honest, trustworthy, and dependable workers. My résumé, of course, was very helpful, but all along it was that first social encounter which had worried me sick for months. In the end, it all worked out and I am very happy and intend to be here for many years."

Rachael: Environmentalist

Rachael has a bachelor's of science degree in ecology and a masters degree in environmental studies but her area of interest, and specialization, involves the environmental removal of toxic substances in general and mercury in particular.

"The average person has no idea how hazardous mercury is or how prevalent it is throughout the environment," Rachael tells me. "Mercury is not just found in vaccines that use the preservative thimerosal, it's everywhere, rocks, soil, water, the air, and once it gets into the earth or water it does not break down, so it poses a major threat to fish, waterfowl, and wildlife as well as humans. It's used as a biocide, an industrial catalyst, and a disinfectant, even though it is an extremely poisonous neurotoxin that gets into the central nervous system and affects all of our senses, particularly during prenatal or early postnatal stages of development."

Although many environmentalists and laypersons are well aware of the dangers of mercury, even at very low levels, Rachael has a personal connection for her passion toward her work with this toxic substance.

"My younger brother," says Rachael, "is low-functioning autistic, and all of us in our family are certain that mercury was the catalyst that sparked off this condition, not only in him, but in me as well. Our family has a number of bright, high-achieving persons scattered throughout so we all come from an excellent gene pool. A number of us, however, like one of my aunts, my grandmother on my father's side, and two cousins, both of whom are engineers, would all fall under the category of Pervasive Development Disorder, if they were ever tested, but they have been successful all of their lives so that issue has never come about. I am fortunate that the result it had on me, the mercury, was that of Asperger's Syndrome, which I think it's an endowment because, with all of its publicized 'deficits,' I see it more as a God-given ability that comes with a lot of tools for survival in the twenty-first century.

"Mercury," Rachael continues, "is everywhere, people who work in paint shops, dentists, industrial laundries, pottery, landfills, laboratories, printing presses, septic systems, and hospitals—mercury can be found in all sorts of unsuspected places in hospitals—crematoriums, fumes at gasoline filling stations, waste incinerators, petroleum refineries, mining, the list is endless. In our own homes, and schools, batteries, thermometers, barometers, light switches, and fluorescent lamps all contain mercury.

"I once saw two young teenagers float two large, fluorescent tubes off into a lake. They pushed them off like small vessels, and once the tubes got about 25–30 meters or so from the shore, they shot at them with pellet rifles, until the tubes exploded, releasing not only the glass, but the mercury vapors into the water. A typical fluorescent lamp contains about 23 milligrams of mercury, which, when released into any bio-system, will have disastrous effects. Once that mercury entered the water, it eventually contaminated a lot of the fish there, fish that will be eventually caught by some unsuspecting person—perhaps even those children themselves, or someone in their family—and the contamination will travel from one living organism to the next.

"I've also heard about people disposing all sorts of toxic materials into lakes and rivers, like car batteries, oil and gasoline, industrial detergents, paint, and all sorts of other waste that can, and will, have lethal conse-quences," Rachael adds. "We have an incredibly monumental task ahead of us and it has to start with educating the public and taking responsibility for our own actions. If we could just get people to make a commitment to recy-cling, continue to press our politicians to set very rigid standards on the use of mercury in our products, and, most importantly, move away from using fossil fuels, that would be a considerable achievement that would give future generations a chance of living in a much safer planet."

> The way these children perceive the world can change and transform the way we see the world and make it a more magical place, full of wonder and variety. Children with ASD can teach us about the infinite variety of sameness, and, in seeing their diversity, we realize that there is a sameness to us all. Once we appreciate this, our attempts to help children with ASD accommodate to our world can be more successful and perhaps accom-plished without the loss of their special gifts. (Szatmari 2004, p.3)

Rachael dedicates her professional and personal life to raising awareness to mercury and other ecological pollutants. Although her job responsibilities involve research and application of safe "green" alternatives, she spends much of her free time conducting free seminars and lectures on these topics. She has spent her past three "two-week vacations" volunteering at agencies that help to coordinate clean up efforts at oil spills, recycling facil-ities, and landfills.

Dennis: Shipping and Receiving Clerk

Forty-eight-year-old Dennis has been working as shipping and receiving clerk for 29 years, all at the same company.

> If you enjoy working with facts, figures and data, you would do well in the accounting and record keeping fields. Precision and a passion for order are what count in these occupations. For many on the autism spectrum, especially nonvisual thinkers, this kind of work can be very fulfilling. ("Sheryl," quoted in Grandin and Duffy 2004, p.112)

"It's not a glamorous job," Dennis says, "but I like it very much."

Dennis can trace his inclination and facility with record keeping back to his early teens when he became his family's "official organizer."

"When I was just 11," Dennis recounts, "I developed this whole, intricate record keeping system for our whole family. The idea started when I noticed my mom scrambling through her purse at the supermarket looking for discount coupons. I remember asking her why she wasn't more organized, and she told me it was because of us kids. The next day I walked up to her while she was fixing supper in the kitchen and handed her a small index card box which I had alphabetized and labeled according to all of the different food groups. This not only became the family's official 'coupon box' but also the first of many such methods of organization that I would continue to develop over the years, including now. One of the happiest days of my life, in fact, was the following tax season when my dad sat me up on his lap and gave me a big hug. 'This is the first time in my life that all of our tax records are in order!' he said. I guess that pretty much sealed my career path for me right then and there.

Today, Dennis continues to be proud of a job well done and his dependability. "I have only taken two sick days over the past 29 years, and that is a record at this company. I have also never been late or had to leave early, except for some emergencies now and then, or when it couldn't be helped, but, mostly, I put in an eight-hour day. If I ever have to leave early for any reason then I work the extra time the next day or two."

Dennis's duties include filling work orders, recording data, filling out requisition forms, maintaining supply inventory, and always keeping a keen eye on storage space. He does not like computers but he has learned to use them and sees that they are helpful although, if it were up to him, he'd go back to doing things "the old fashioned way."

Dennis, who has never been married, shares an apartment with a friend. His hobbies include fishing, crossword puzzles, and hiking.

Garrett: Physics Researcher

Having just celebrated his thirty-ninth birthday, Garrett feels he has a unique position at the "cutting edge" of one the frontiers of physics: nanomagnetics.

Garrett, a researcher, is currently involved in investigating the enhanced magnetocaloric effect in magnetic nanocomposites and the applications of magneto-optic imaging film techniques in their relation to high-density magnetic recording media. He is further collecting data on spin dynamics and condensed matter theory.

"When I was growing up," Garrett states, "I loved brainteasers, back-gammon, chess, what most people would call brainy type games. I am a self-confessed, hopeless 'Trekkie,' I guess, and maybe even a nerd, but I think that's a cool thing to be now. Either way, that's who I am and I don't really care what anyone else thinks about it! I love playing games like 'Dune,' 'Starcraft,' 'Sid Meier,' and the like."

Garrett traces his interest in physics to his early college days when he would spend his free time reading about wave particles, string theory, and quantum phenomena. A couple of his side interests at this time, in fact, relate to semiconductor quantum structures and micromagnetic simulational work.

Although Garrett indicates he has little time for socializing, he does enjoy playing computer games and surfing the web for fresh innovations. His work, he indicates, also gives him the opportunity to travel. Most recently, he attended the International Workshop on Nanomagnetism, which was held in Havana, Cuba, in November of 2004, where he got to present an abstract as well as hear lectures by luminaries on his topics of interest from all around the world, including speakers from Spain, Brazil, Japan, and Germany. Earlier, in February of 2004, he also enjoyed the opportunity to attend the NSF Workshop on Nanotechnology at the Rochester Institute of Technology, which is a lot closer to home, and where he had the opportunity to speak with a number of high school students about careers in physics while considering majors in nanotechnology.

> On tests of intuitive physics, males score higher than females, and people with AS score higher than males…math is frequently chosen by people with AS as their favorite subject at school…boys prefer constructional and vehicle toys more than girls do, and children with autism or AS often have this toy preference very strongly…many people with AS pursue mechanics and computing as their major leisure interests. (Baron-Cohen 2003, p.152)

Vanna: Librarian

Fifty-two-year-old Vanna has been working as a full-time public librarian for the past 27 years. She earned a master's degree in library science after returning to school 17 years ago. Since then she has continued her training in order to stay abreast of the rapidly emerging trends in technology, such as advanced media, the Internet, virtual libraries, and remote access.

Vanna enjoys dividing her time up between the three primary areas of library work: administrative, technical, and user services. Her favorite duties, however, involve classifying and cataloging new arrivals, classifying information, acquisitions, and special collections. Her self-professed "guilty pleasures" include sorting through rare books and genealogy.

Vanna fell in love with libraries in the sixth grade at a time that she describes as "needing a safe haven" from all of the commotion going on all around her at school. Being hyperlexic (a precocious reader with a love of words and letters)—she began reading sometime around the age of two or three—she has found an affinity to the written and printed word, and reading, throughout her life. In effect, she feels that the marriage between herself and library work was one that was cemented from birth.

Vanna feels that beyond providing a place of employment and a safe haven, libraries afford a perfect environment for people throughout the high end of the autism spectrum, as it gives them a central place where they can either be alone or socialize with others who share similar interests at their own pace. One of her concerns, in fact, is that future, online libraries may eventually replace brick and mortar locations that afford such perfect sanctuaries for so many people, Aspies or not, over so many years.

> One's interest and commitment to a subject, coupled with perseverance, make research very attractive. Laboratory-based work in medical and pharmaceutical settings is equally interesting and makes effective use of intellectual strengths. Outside of direct academic research, employment based on record keeping or bookkeeping also leans on the strengths of AS. A library requires staff that have a good sense of order, neatness and fastidious attention to detail. Bookkeeping needs people who are capable of applying rules consistently, and have a fondness for neatness and detail. (Harpur *et al.* 2003, p.257)

Tom: Agricultural Worker

Forty-one-year-old Tom works in a greenhouse. His "vocational path" began at age 12 while working with his father who had his own landscaping business. Tom discovered greenhouses during his sophomore year in high school and "became addicted to them because they were like stepping into a different dimension where everything was healthy and serene."

"Being around plants is very soothing and healing," Tom says. "They don't have any expectations of you and appreciate everything you do for them with a quiet gracefulness. Throughout my life, whenever I feel stressed, upset, or a little down, I can always go around plants and within minutes everything is all right.

"Aside from the healing serenity that I get from working in a greenhouse," Tom adds, "I also love the actual work, which I see more as a hobby, than a job. My favorite things to do are staking trees, packing plants, and pruning. I have always wanted to learn about Japanese bonsais and may still do that someday.

"I think that the fact that I have Asperger's, which I only found out a few years ago, much to my relief, helps me in a lot of ways in my work. Having Asperger's I am not much of a people person because I really don't know what to say or do when I am around people. I have always felt much more comfortable being around plants. Actually, I feel that plants are easier to communicate with than people. I think there are a lot of ways in which plants, trees, and flowers can tell us when they are sad or stressed, or when they have been abused or neglected, in the same way that animals can. I think that getting paid for being a 'plant nurturer' makes me a very lucky man."

> If you recognize and nurture their talents and provide them with appropriate interventions and support students with AS have the potential to make astonishing achievements. All have the potential to find fulfillment and happiness along the way. (Moore 2002, p.45)

Jeremy: Landscape Architect

Thirty-one-year-old Jeremy is a self-employed landscape architect. His employers have included real estate developers, banks, nursing homes, and schools, but his favorite type of work involves what he describes as "road-rage minimization" or traffic calming. Jeremy describes this type of work "sort of like an artist painting relaxing scenes with the roadway shoulders being a giant canvas.

"Our goal," he notes, "is not only to improve the aesthetic of the roadways, so that drivers can enjoy the scenery, but to hopefully get the people to slow down and look at the flowers, or trees, or greenery, the whole environment around them as they drive on for miles and miles. Driving can get pretty monotonous, so if you have aesthetically pleasing environments surrounding you I think that tends to make people feel a lot happier, and maybe be kind to each other a little more.

"A lot of our time is spent inside an office, which I don't particularly like," Jeremy shares, "but that's where it all begins, all the planning, designing, especially now because we use a lot of computer software and computer simulations, which I love, because I love working on computers. I guess I have the perfect job because I get to do the two things I love best, helping to create beautiful environments and playing on computers!"

> Temple constantly runs "simulations," as she calls them, in her head: "I visualize the animal entering the chute, from different angles, different distances, zooming in or wide angle, even from a helicopter view—or I turn myself into an animal, and feel what it would feel entering the chute." (Sacks 1995, p.267)

Verne: Proofreader

"I began proofreading, I think, from the time I was born," 27-year-old Verne confides. "My mother is always telling people that I probably corrected the attending physician's name on his name tag when I came out of the womb."

"Super-reader" Verne, which he proudly claims as his moniker, is just that—a "super-reader." He can read extremely fast and prides himself on "catching typos...especially from people who are supposed to be my superiors. It's amazing how many errors there are everywhere: supermarkets, restaurants, businesses, doctors' offices, highway road signs, schools, universities, even libraries! I've always loved pointing out the errors, ever since I learned to speak. Actually, just the other day I spotted how someone had received an award from their district and the plaque read: 'D-i-s-r-t-i-c-t'! That sort of thing cracks me up."

Verne says he loves every aspect of his job and is always in search of "new words, and rare, archaic spellings." He speaks seven languages fluently—English, French, German, Spanish, Greek, Portuguese, and Italian—but is learning Japanese and wants to learn as many languages as possible. He keeps a running record of the "funniest misspellings ever," and carries a digital camera around with him as often as possible so that he can take pictures of printed goof-ups. He hopes to write a book "before I'm 30" that would pull together his collection that also includes "document omissions, inconsistencies, typing errors, grammatical mistakes, ridiculous punctuations," and just about everything one can imagine having to do with the "mis-written form."

> The fact that I excelled at certain tasks—keeping records, making keen observations, descriptively communicating information, and memorizing events perfectly—not only saved me but deposited me exactly where I wanted to be. (Prince-Hughes 2002, pp.103–4).

Norman: Forensic Science Analyst

Norman, 39 years old, describes himself as a "natural born" forensic scientist and criminologist who began his "apprenticeship" by reading crime and mystery comics, then progressed to novels and real-life studies by the time he was in early high school.

"I was the only kid I ever knew of in high school," Norman says, "who would go to the college library after school to look up research on new developments on things like ballistics, fingerprinting, handwriting analysis, things like that. I got a 'lab' for my tenth birthday and that was probably the best gift of my life. I remember going around taking everyone's fingerprints and then cataloging them. When I was 12 I got my first camera and what I would do was have my friends, younger brother and sister, relatives, and whoever would go along with it, pose like corpses who had been shot, then take pictures of them for identification. Kids in school would sometimes really get into it and they would try to come up with new ways that someone could fall after being shot or stabbed."

Norman believes that his "strong, visual learning style" has been very helpful in his development as a forensic scientist. "I have always used visual aides naturally to teach myself. Colors, pictures, charts, drawings, matrices, and diagrams to help me to visualize all of the different links and pathways between system components. These visually oriented approaches have always been helpful. I think that being a visual-oriented learner is a tremendous advantage in my line of work."

Among his favorite duties, Norman lists reconstructing crime scenes, using computer software to decipher altered evidence, identifying rare drugs and lethal substances, and, most of all, "noticing little things that no one else does."

> Some adults with AS are fascinated by crime reports because they enjoy working out basic rules of the following kind: if the victim showed physical signs a, b, and c, then the murder in all likelihood involved techniques x, y, and z. (Baron-Cohen 2003, p.148)

According to Norman he has been his department's "last hope" for seven years running, a title which he proudly adheres to. "When I first came into the agency," he indicates, "everyone just thought I was a weird geek, but now, now I'm the most respected person there. I'm still a geek, I think that's a good thing, like Cuomo from Weezer [Rivers

Cuomo, the lead singer of a popular music group], but everyone respects me and when there is something that no one else can figure out, then I'm the man."

Citing "the classic Batman" as his "absolutely no doubt about it world's greatest criminologist ever," he adds, "sometimes I think I should wear a cape."

Dahlia: Medical Transcriptionist

Dahlia is a 25-year-old medical transcriptionist who has worked at a large medical clinic over the past two years.

She feels that her job is one that helps her mind "stay in shape just like exercising your body will help to keep it in shape." She feels that her duties, which include responsibilities such as always staying updated in anatomy, medicine, physiology, medical jargon, abbreviations, and drug names, make for "a total brain workout."

"I've always heard how Aspies are supposed to be mostly visual thinkers, but I think that I have a strong auditory thinking style, although I learn visually as well. Making up mnemonics, for instance, I think that would be a combination of a visual and auditory thinking style. One of the ways that I teach myself different words, rules, clinical and medical terms, and just about anything else is by creating acronyms, focusing on the first letter of the words to come up with some contextual reference to the meaning or to make it somehow memorable or significant to myself.

"I have always had very good focusing abilities, and can hone in to things like a laser so when I'm working I'm there 100 percent and when I'm listening I just connect to the dictated transcript and perform data entry and I rarely have to rewind or replay anything unless it is garbled. I pride myself on never making any mistakes in grammar, spelling, or punctuation. I guess my specialty is knowing or deciphering abbreviations because everyone always comes to me when they need help with them. Once I learn something, like a spelling or abbreviation, I tend to never forget them. It's almost as if I can put my mind in some sort of search mode, visually type in a word, and then my brain just finds it. It's very cool! My dad always said he could do that so I guess I got it from him."

> At first I wrote classical music. I could not read sheet music…I had simply to remember my pieces…as these pieces became more complex, I developed a strategy of writing down timing using a series of dots and dashes of differing lengths, and learned to write the pitch over these dots and dashes using their letter names and arrows showing whether they went up or down in pitch. (Williams 1992, p.127)

Ollie: Meter Reader

The thing that Ollie, who is 27 years old, likes most about being a utilities meter reader is that it gives him time to be on his own. "I'm not much for socializing and chatting," he explains, "but I like being out and about and being thorough in everything I do."

> An AS person is more likely to think, "The law says I can't break into a house so I won't do it." We like rules. Rules make things easier to understand. Rules are clear. Rules are secure. AS people are a lot more rigid in their thoughts than other people. (Jackson 2002, p.183)

As for the favorite part of his actual work duties, Ollie enjoys locating "hard-to-find things like factory defects, loose connections, broken seals. Those are the things that make the job fun. There are people who also try to cheat the meters, and they find ways of doing it, but you can figure it out, which is a good feeling, almost like being a detective. A couple of times this one person's meter actually went 'back in time,' his reading was actually lower than the month before, so he, like, really overdid it, or under-did it. So that was not very smart. But almost everyone else is honest so it's just a matter of making the rounds and doing a day's work. It's a great job."

Sabina: FX Artist

Twenty-six-year-old Sabina prides herself on being the only female in her company of 27 employees who is not engaged in some sort of secretarial duty. Her educational background includes computer animation, 3D modeling, film, and video. She can work with any number of 3D packages such as MAX, Softimage, 3DS, and Maya, and loves 3D architecture and manipulating animation. She feels that the experience she's gained over the past year in MEL scripting has helped to guarantee her a place with her current company "for at least the next few months." She would like to gain more experience with particle effects and systems, custom tools, and shaders. She has a bachelor's degree in computer science and is nearing completion on a master's degree.

"I am most definitely a visual person," Sabina observes. "I am also an incredible spatial learner. I think I am one of those people who has an internal gyroscope. You can literally put a brown paper bag over my head, spin me around, and I will start walking off, or driving, in the right direction. Even as a little girl I was always coming up with ways of improving photographs, videos, always manipulating visual images in my mind.

"I most enjoy creating futuristic, alien environments, multidimensional characters from future generations, cinematics, and creating visceral effects. The main thing I would like to see in computer games, however, is stronger female characters, slick and sexy, yes, but independent and progressive minded as well. How about a flat-chested, feminist super-heroine whose powers involve saving animals from bullies?

"I have the Aspie work ethic, the ol', 'highly focused beam of synchronized single-wavelength radiation' thing going on; it can get pretty scary, and so can my work, so, look out!"

> My imagination works like the computer graphics programs that created the lifelike dinosaurs in *Jurassic Park*. When I do an equipment simulation in my imagination or work on an engineering simulation in my imagination or work on an engineering problem, it is like seeing it on a videotape in my mind. I can view it from any angle, placing myself above or below the equipment and rotating it at the same time. I don't need a fancy graphics program that can produce three-dimensional design simulations. I can do it better and faster in my head. (Grandin 1995, p.21)

Ea: Game Programmer and Developer

Ea, who is 22 years old, describes himself as a "mastermind" game programmer who grew up "destroying my older brothers' games so that I could make them better. Essentially, I was a computer child prodigy." His father, who was working as a computer programmer and game developer before Ea was born used to write games in Turbo Pascal and work on a Want 2000 business computer using BASIC language. Ea got his first experience "playing around with an old Commodore PET and an Amiga 1000," which he still keeps around as he describes himself as someone who just can't throw anything away. He has a BS in computer engineering.

> They [people with AS] frequently describe their brains as being just like computers—either containing some piece of information or not. In other words, they think in a way that is binary, digital, and precise; they do not think in approximations in the same way that many other people do. In a recent book about an artist with AS, Sally Wheelwright and I coined a phrase for this: "the exact mind." (Baron-Cohen 2003, pp.147–8)

"Back in grade school," Ea recalls, "I loved performing complex calculations on what other people thought were incredible bits of data. I'd challenge other kids to race me using calculators or whatever they had around, and I'd always win. I was one of those weird kids who thought trig and algebra, and later physics and statistics, were more about games with tricks and shortcuts than subjects one should be graded on."

Ea, who describes himself as both a visual and logical thinker, currently develops games for Playstation, Xbox, PSP, GameCube, and "anything else they can throw at me."

"I love upgrading, writing, and debugging code," Ea states. "It's all about the next generation, if you stop for lunch, you missed it, by the time you get back they've morphed into the next stage. It's like walking out in the middle of a movie to get popcorn, you get back and someone has to catch you up, then you missed what happened while they were catching you up."

Ea feels comfortable with 3D acceleration, MIPS, graphics, BREW, Perl, compression schemes, object-oriented methodologies, PHP, Java, and C/C++ but confesses that most of his worthwhile skills are self-taught, "a result of late night experimentation. I probably average like two, two and one-half hours of sleep per night, and even then I usually dream about new games." His favorite pastime is inventing games for hand-held devices.

Larry: Surveyor

(The following transcript appears verbatim as contributed by Larry.)

My name is Larry. I do have Asperger's Syndrome, it was officially diagnosed three years ago and that helped me to understand myself a lot better than I had before. It also helped me to understand that being different like myself is neither good or bad, because if everyone were the same the world would be a very boring place. I also now realize that many of the things I have been able to do since I was a young boy, like drawing very clear maps, being very picky about having things done just right, and being very concerned with accurate measurements has helped me to become successful at my job and in my life. I am 37 years old and I work as a county surveyor. I am married to a woman who is a nurse practitioner and we have two sons, ages seven and five. My work involves writing descriptions of property boundary surveys, planning and conducting land surveys, establishing baselines and elevations, and performing various geodetic measurements. At times, I am called upon to search through registries for legal records and land titles particularly when there are discrepancies regarding property boundaries. Some of my work involves preparing and designing maps, reports, sketches, and descriptions of surveys. Verification of data accuracy is one of the most essential parts of my job, as measurements and calculations have to be done very specifically so as not to cheat a property owner or land developer from protected land dimensions, property lines, or legal boundaries. The calculation of land features and terrain, including contour, elevation, relative positions, depth, and viability of the land in relation to building purposes, is an exact science that has to be skillfully made by competent, experienced professionals. I consider myself a competent, capable surveyor who prides himself on his work. I am honored to take part in this survey and only ask that you reproduce this material exactly as I have written it.

> What intrigued me about the possibility that Sharon had AS was not only the types of social difficulties she described but also that she was an architect. This obviously required a high degree of perceptual skill and a penchant for seeing visual nuance and detail… She wrote that people who are good at social interactions are often quite blind to physical reality: "Organizations are filled with people who are socially adept, yet they seem to be as blind to the material world as those with autism are to social reality. In physical reality, the existence of things cannot be denied." (Szatmari 2004, pp.60–1)

Adam: Stamp and Coin Collector

As it sometimes occurs at one point or another during many people's life-times, Adam's initial career innovation occurred by happenstance. In his case, this "moment of happenstance" arrived on a Tuesday during summer school break.

On what he describes as "the day of omens" the then seven-year-old Adam and his older brother, Ralphie, walked up to a vendor and purchased two ice cream cones. As each brother paid for their own summer treats, Adam, who had the reputation for "noticing everything," and habitually counted his change very carefully, noticed that one of the pennies he had received back from the ice cream vendor was rather unusual.

"At first," the now 45-year-old collectible store proprietor recalls, "I just thought it was a Canadian penny, which I didn't like because my grandfather always used to tell us that their currency was worth less than U.S. currency. When I looked at it a little closer, however, I noticed that the coin clearly noted the inscription, 'United States of America' with the words evenly divided in a semi-circle around an American Indian's profile. In the rear, the coin bore the inscription, 'one cent' inscribed within a laurel and underneath what looked like a small emblem or a harp. Most intriguing of all, however, was the fact that, underneath the profile of the American Indian, the coin had the date: '1905'!

"I immediately showed this coin to my brother, Ralphie," a very excited Adam continued, "who insisted that, being older, he had the right to the coin. I grabbed that coin inside of my hand and made the tightest fist I possibly could, as Ralphie was a lot stronger than I, and then ran home as fast as I could. If I could just get home before Ralphie could wrestle that magical coin away from me, and tell our mom about my find, that would secure my legal right to this 'one of a kind' coin. Having shown it our mother, however, she sort of deflated my excitement by assuring me that it was, indeed, an American coin, but also letting me know that there were likely millions more floating around the country.

"Nonetheless, to me, a coin from 1905 was just about as cool as having a moon rock, or dust from one of Saturn's rings, or something like that, so I placed it in my special 'finder's box,' and considered it a treasure.

"Later that same night," Adam told me, "while sitting around the dinner table our mom and dad, inspired by my 1905 Indian head penny, told us stories about other coins that used to be common finds when they were our age. Coins like 'buffalo head nickels,' and 'liberty head quarters,' and the like. She then pulled out an old box that contained a stack of old letters she had kept over the years, some that dad had sent while away on business, others that our grandparents had sent one another during the war. Most special of all, what caught my seven-year-old wanderlust eye was a postcard that featured a first day, 'Win the War!' stamp from 1942 and the classic portrait of 'Uncle Sam' flanked by the slogan, 'I'm Working with Uncle Sam!' What really hit it out of the park for me, however, was that the stamp had been cancelled on August 12, 1942. Seeing that 'ancient' date sent my mind reeling. On that fateful 'day of omens,' when the 1942 stamp and 1905 coin came together, my career goal was sealed. From then on I switched my 'obsession,' or at least partly, from subway trains and railroad cars to coin and stamp collecting."

At the age of 17, Adam, who describes himself as "shy, quirky and pretty obsessive, but with a remarkable eye for detail" impressed the local owner of a coin and stamp collector's store with his encyclopedic knowledge and secured a part-time job after school and on weekends. That job, Adam recalls, became his "social oasis." Having little in common with most of his peers, the job not only gave him something productive to focus on, but provided an income that he could use to seriously pursue his collecting hobby.

Today, Adam is the proud owner of his own collectible store. Although through the years he has made countless impressive finds, Adam still displays the now professionally framed 1905 Indian head penny and 1942 World War II stamp in a special spot inside the store's main display case.

> AS involves a different kind of intelligence. The strong drive to systemize means that the person with AS becomes a *specialist* in something, or even in everything they delve into… The systemizing drive in AS is often a drive to identify the *underlying structure* in the world. (Baron-Cohen 2003, p.149)

Indicating that his "superior eye for detail, extreme patience, and obsessive pursuit of certain items" has made him sort of a "numismatic and philatelist superhero," Adam still becomes very excited when he holds his ever changing "favorites" as he encounters them over the years.

At this point in time, his "serious" pursuits involve "flawed coins," with his recent favorite coin-related finds including a "2005-D, all bald bison nickel, and a 1999 New Jersey quarter which is missing the letters 's' and 'r' in the center of the word, 'Cros*sr*oads.'" His ongoing favorite over the past few years continues to be "any and all Sacagawea dollars," and his long-time favorite collectibles include transit (railway, subway) tokens and colonial coins, which brings together two of his strongest lifelong passions, subway trains and coins. His overall favorite at the moment, however, is a nearly mint, 1791 colonial farthing halfpenny that he spotted in a cashier's drawer at a grocer. "The woman thought it was a Canadian penny!" Adam shares with absolute delight.

Regarding what he describes as his "silly" favorites, Adam smiles slyly, and tells of his "other passion—everything Star Wars," and shares his excitement over his Star Wars Silver Commemorative Stamp, Star Wars classic vehicles of the saga, and Star Wars trilogy commemorative collector sets. Although he realizes that the actual financial worth of his "silly passions," will never "pay the bills," he adds that retirement will be a lot sweeter as long as he holds on to "priceless trinkets" such as his "Star Wars set of three-credit coins: the Bronze, 1000 credit Ord Mantell, the Silver 1000 credit Bespin, and the Gold, 1000 credit Alderaan pieces."

Always in quest of "digging up new treasure troves," Adam's active membership in a number of organizations, such as the American Numismatic and the Graphics Philately Associations, have provided him with a circle of friends from all over the world whom he considers his "soul mates" and extended family.

Jason: Comic Book Store Manager

Twenty-two-year-old Jason loves comics. Actually, his favorite picture, which rests upon the mantel of his parents' fireplace in the family living room, shows the precocious reader, aged three, reading an old *Archie* comic.

"I always read everything," Jason states. "It doesn't matter what it is, roadway signs, information on pill bottles, advertisements that they stick in magazines, register receipts, everything."

"When I get a new CD, for instance," Jason adds, "I always have to read the booklet that comes inside first, before I listen to it. And if it doesn't have any words in it, just pictures, well, it's just really annoying and it kind of ruins it for me. The best thing is when you can read the lyrics while they sing."

Jason's love of reading, in fact, is so intense that he actually prefers to watch movies with the captions on so that he can read the dialogue as he watches them.

Jason's primary infatuation, however, is with comics and he is intent on making a career out of his passion. Well on the road to fulfilling this vocational ambition, he is currently the manager at a comic book store where he has worked since his fifteenth birthday.

"I used to get all of my comics at this store when I was a little kid," Jason recalls as a look of elation shines across his face, "and I used to spend hours there, sitting on the floor reading all the comics I couldn't afford, 'cause I was a little kid. But even then I used to know more than the people who worked there."

When Jason was just 12, in fact, the store's owner began to turn to him as an "amateur consultant" regarding what comics and related paraphernalia he should be stocking to bring and satisfy the savvy customers. Jason was happy to oblige. His fee was "two free comics per week." Even at the age of 12, then, Jason was well on his career path as a comic industrialist.

Adroitly displaying his zeal and expertise regarding everything "comics," Jason regales the listener with an interesting, detailed lecture of comic book history. Although he cites the "incomparable" Golden Age (1938–1955) as his favorite comic book era, he is just as well versed in "other" eras, such as the Silver (1956–1969), Bronze (1970–1979), and current, Modern Age (1980 to the present), citing the latter as "of very little interest." These more current comics, he feels, "are the same as movies that are nothing but special effects," and have no real substance to them.

"The older comics were all about art and soul," he indicates. "These new ones are all about making money."

Among Golden Age genres, Jason's favorites include superheroes, horror, war, sci-fi, and cartoon characters. When asked about his all-time-favorite comic, Jason becomes seriously pensive and asks me to "give him a minute to collect his thoughts." After a brief "scan of his database" (as he refers to the information in his brain) he almost screams out, "*World's Finest Comics* 30, firefighter fire truck issue!" Asked why this is a noted favorite, Jason quickly indicates that this particular comic's "perfect cover" features the trio of Superman, Batman, and Robin riding a red (his favorite color) fire truck (his favorite vehicle), and—with an extra spark of excitement he adds—"Robin is at the wheel!" Looking at me with an impish smile, the 22-year-old's child-like spirit shines through as he throws both of his hands up in a gesture of unrestrained excitement and exclaims, "Can you imagine?!"

Asked what his "dream acquisition" would be, he sighs, looks straight up, slumps down on his chair, and sighs, "Well, of course, it would be the Action Comics *Superman* #1 through #10 1938 series."

As Jason follows up his personal "holy grail of all comics" with a lengthy discussion of how Action Comics, which was originally Detective Comics, then National Comics, and then National Periodical Publications before becoming the current "DC Comics" was the series that initially introduced Superman as "the first and ultimate superhero" (although he actually prefers Batman as he is a "regular guy" who has to make do with his wits rather than alien superpowers), and how Action Comics have, as of 2005, released over 800 comics, and how "Action #1 is the source of Superman's true origins," I sit and marvel over a young man who, by the very young age of 22 has not only already realized many of his life's dreams, but is fully content with his place in the universe.

> Elizabeth Anderson and Pauline Emmons [sensory dysfunction authors] view their SD [sensory disordered] children as superheroes because of the "strength and courage it takes for them to cope with their disorder." (Huebner 2001, p.476)

Dierdra: Paralegal/Legal Assistant

Currently attending law school, Dierdra is "making ends meet" with her current job as a paralegal. As she describes her work and job descriptions, the 28-year-old emphasizes how a lot of the work that many people think attorneys perform is actually delegated to, and carried out, by legal assistants like herself.

"Just about anything that doesn't fall under actual 'practicing law'," she says, "which includes things like giving out legal advice, presenting cases in court, or setting legal fees is fair game for us."

Diagnosed with AS just a few years ago—a realization that she feels turned her life around for the better—Dierdra feels that a lot of her "Aspie-type skills" have helped her tremendously along her career path. "Not so much socially," she indicates, "but, professionally, I think that being an Aspie is really a plus once you find your niche."

> Like other gifted children, those with AS can show a high level of moral development. Their concepts of fairness and justice can be advanced, and they can adhere to high ideals of following rules, being honest and fair. (Lovecky 2004, p.145)

Among her "Aspie skills," Dierdra regards her remarkable memory—which never fails to amaze the law partners at the firm—eye for detail, innate ability to "notice little things that most other people seem to miss," a sense of "comfortable emotional detachment," and a total sense of responsibility as strong professional advantages. Additionally, she cites her affinity for and "personal relationship" with computers and her technical know-how of constantly emerging software packages and the Internet, as factors that "really distance myself from the other paralegals, and specially the attorneys, in the firm." She also feels that her superior ability to scan documents rapidly, as well as decipher and upgrade software programs, are due to her "Aspie brain."

"Even the Aspie things that I struggle with have really become strengths," Dierdra indicates. "I think the fact that I have always struggled with things like organization and multitasking has helped me to become a very organized person who has learned how to juggle lots of things at once. In my mind, I see myself not juggling a lot of things, but rather like one of those people who spins a number of plates on top of a tall, thin pole and keeps them from falling by being able to zero in on the plates and nothing but the plates, and making sure they all keep spinning and never fall. I remember seeing someone doing that in an old, 'Nick at Night' segment of some 1950s variety TV show and that's a helpful image."

Very much in tune with "people's rights" Dierdra cites "labor laws and employee benefits" as two of her primary interests. She is further interested in community legal-service projects that would target assisting the poor, handicapped, aged, and others who are often discriminated against and have little or no resources to pay for their legal counsel, or the ability or education to fully comprehend what they are entitled to by virtue of existing laws.

Paolo: Statistician

Paolo's love of statistics began at the tender age of ten, when he and his uncle used to sit in front of the television, watching baseball games and figuring out the statistics of each player's batting average as they either got a base hit, struck out, walked, or reached on an error. Until then, the boy's parents had been unable to get the young boy excited about sports or anything else that could help him to connect with his peers. By noticing the boy's love of numbers and talent for calculating data, however, Paolo's uncle had hit upon a splendid way of both reducing the family concerns regarding the boy's "troublesome and unproductive obsessions," while getting him interested in an area where he could better relate to his sport-loving peers.

By the age of 12, Paolo had progressed to sophisticated methods of statistical probability and had memorized an impressive number of formulas and equations that, as they later learned, are typically not introduced until the university level. Soon, young Paolo was applying statistical analysis to everything from assisting his mother in figuring out how many calories and carbohydrates she should eat each day to maintain her weight, to advising his dad on investments.

> Many persons with Asperger's Syndrome are academically successful and attend college. The student's intellectual ability, the severity of the person's behavioral challenges, and the availability of a personal support system appear to be factors in determining academic success. The focused nature of academics or research can be a good career fit for persons dedicated to compiling an exhaustive database of information on any particular subject. Bright persons with AS may develop their focused interests into science and computer-related vocations. Fact and detail-based jobs are another way of achieving a good fit between the person with AS and a career. (Henderson 2000, p.31)

Today, at the young age of 27, Paolo is a freelance, professional statistician and consultant conducting scientific research in areas ranging from field experiments for irrigation plants and ecological quality measurements, to conducting clinical trials to help determine the effectiveness of various medications. As a hobby, Paolo also relies on statistics as he tries to predict consumer price patterns, fluctuations in the market, and—his personal favorite—weather forecasting. His self-proclaimed "Aspie-enhanced" skills help him to manage, and continually improve upon, both his family's and his own investment portfolios.

Bjorn: Military Engineer

When he was growing up, Bjorn excelled at mapmaking, code breaking, and sketching 3D drawings. He also loved watching war movies although, rather than focusing on the battles, he would instead notice details others would completely miss, such as the landscape configurations, length of the airfields, and strategic locations of buildings, roads, hills, lakes, and other environmental factors. In essence, he felt that these were details that "helped to really determine not only whether the movie was realistic or not, but also gave the military component with a keen eye the clear advantage."

In school, no matter what the assignment was, everything that Bjorn did somehow found a connection with strategies that involved physical strategies, deciphering "hidden codes," and the manipulation of "three-dimensional nature" to gain an advantage over his competitors.

"Whether an assignment had anything to do with it or not," Bjorn boasts, "I would always find a way to visually present the information by drawing 3D sketches that always involved making the most out of the available geography, time of day, season of the year, and other things like that. Also, any presentations I did always had hidden codes that the other kids, and the teacher, would have to try and figure out but they never could. Ironically, that was both fun as well as a waste of time."

Judging from his lifelong self-teachings and personal fixations, Bjorn's career path was also one that most would have seen as rather predictable. Although Bjorn initially began his career working in military intelligence— intercepting foreign military communications, deciphering military codes, and studying intelligence reports, maps, and charts of alien territories—he eventually moved into nuclear engineering.

As such, the very bright and intense 32-year-old is now a nuclear engineer in the military with a specialty on designing nuclear submarines and enhancing safety procedures for the handling of nuclear weapons, as well as more effective ways of designing and utilizing nuclear technology. A personal leaning, however, is toward simplifying complicated, time-consuming research projects and developing policies for the safe and proper maintenance of nuclear power plants.

"There are a lot of Aspies in the armed forces," Bjorn adds. "Based on what I have learned and read about Aspies apart from myself, I think that, as a group, we tend to be very rational, peaceful people. So, whether our branch of service is in the Army, Navy, Marines, Air Force, or Coast Guard,

I think it bodes well that many of us tend to lean toward these discipline and rule-based systems that pretty much provide a configuration for our day to day activities. In other words, I think that a lot of us benefit from having the rules and structure that the military provides."

Wrapping up our discussion, Bjorn states that "during the years I have worked in the armed forces I have met many Aspies, and whatever the job, the part we play, at least among the Aspies I've gotten to know, is always one of developing systems to try and ensure peace and being in harmony between ourselves—whether in our country or alien soil—and the world we live in as a whole."

> My time in an army training camp provided me with a structured setting where I knew exactly what was expected from me... The army also provided a structured social environment... I found it easier to relate to others when there was a strict social protocol to follow... I felt a part of the group as we were all going through the same struggle and we were working towards the same goal... Socially, the army helped me in many ways because it forced me to be social, to be assertive, and to take charge even when I didn't want to. ("Donna," quoted in Stoddart 2005, p.341)

> To our amazement, we have seen that autistic individuals, as long as they are intellectually intact, can almost always achieve professional success, usually in highly specialized academic professions, often in very high positions, with a preference for abstract content. We found a large number of people whose mathematical ability determines their professions: mathematicians, technologists, industrial chemists and high-ranking civil servants. (Asperger 1991, p.89)

CHAPTER 4

Notable Persons with Asperger's Syndrome Phenotypes

The notion of a broad Asperger's Syndrome, or autistic, phenotype is one that has garnered interest over the past few years as research focusing on this topic has indicated a number of descriptive similarities that tend to exist between children with these conditions and their parents and other relatives.

Similarities between children with Asperger's Syndrome, and their fathers in particular, has particularly garnered increasing interest from both researchers and clinicians trying to unravel the environmental and neurobiological connections, and genetic markers, that may lead to a broader understanding of these puzzling conditions. Some of the research pertaining to the broad Asperger's/autistic phenotype has extended to examining those characteristics that are typically associated with these populations as exhibited by a number of popular historical characters such as Isaac Newton, Albert Einstein, Lewis Carroll, Nicola Tesla, and many others based on biographies, accounts of acquaintances, or other documentation considered well founded. Similar intellectual excursions are also venturing into what some feel are "Asperger-like traits" of currently popular persons with whom the general public is familiar, and some well-known persons who have openly identified themselves as sharing these traits, or "phenotypes." Extending this reasoning to more current and directly accessible evidence, research has also focused on the parallel occurrence of these genetic–environmentally-based connections between persons presenting with diagnosable criteria for Asperger's or autism, and their family members or relatives (fathers, mothers, siblings, aunts, uncles, grandparents).

In essence, these phenotypes are personal characteristics, or "markers," that can be interpreted as falling somewhere between those apparent in individuals with autism or Asperger's, and other persons characterized as "normal" or "neurotypical" (persons outside of the autism spectrum). Another way of explaining the notion of an Asperger's/autism phenotype would be to describe such characteristics as falling in a gray area, or as "bridging the gap" between persons who would qualify for a diagnosis of Asperger's Syndrome, or autism, and those who share some of these traits but not to the extent that would yield a formal clinical diagnosis. We can note these phenotypes among persons who have distinguished themselves historically, or simply managed to overcome these distinctive ways of being by virtue of their talents, perseverance, and/or intelligence, and/or through the support, nurturing and understanding of others throughout different stages of their lives. These are individuals who, despite these apparent "limitations," have risen to the occasion and managed to turn their "deficits" or "liabilities" into vocational and personal strengths.

Although many of these "phenotypes" fall into visual-spatial, or sensory-motor areas, they can refer to almost any aspect of an individual's personal attributes that tend to set them apart from their "neurotypical" (or, again, "normally functioning") peers. Some of these distinguishing features include:

- being clumsy or awkward

- having "two left feet"

- being "all thumbs"

- preferring, or being best at, exploring the world verbally, rather than physically

- tending to process certain types of information, whether visual, auditory or kinesthetic, slowly but carefully and judiciously

- having poor hand-to-eye, gross-motor or fine-finger coordination

- having problems interacting or communicating in social situations

- being arrhythmic

- seeming to have difficulties making direct eye-contact

- having poor body posture

- being uncomfortable in social situations

- being more comfortable in one-to-one social encounters than among groups

- having problems with direction or handwriting

- tending to have distinctive arousal states (is either hyper- and/or hypo-sensitive or focused, depending on various sensory triggers, the surrounding environment, or topic of interest)

- having problems with, or being unable completely to understand personal boundaries

- in general, sharing a number of the *positive* attributes, traits or characteristics typically associated with Asperger's Syndrome that often contribute to the attainment of remarkable intellectual accomplishments, brilliant discoveries, and outstanding success in a particular field. Some of these include diligence, astute attention to detail, perseverance, unique ways of looking at presenting challenges, extreme patience when engaged in preferred topics or fields of work, and otherwise extraordinary abilities that may not reflect in other—typically social—aspects of their lives.

The "notable historical persons" described in this chapter are among some of the many whose lives and distinctive features researchers and clinicians have explored and written about over the past few years. Although, as these writers consistently point out, it is impossible to formally diagnose someone post mortem (or, in the case of those still living, without under-going a formal diagnostic assessment), it is possible, through careful exam-ination of existing records, to ascertain the extent to which many of these remarkable characters have been (or are being) described across various sources as possessing some of the traits or qualities—such as the ones described above—that are features of Asperger's or autism spectrum con-ditions. This points to the possibility that they may fall somewhere on the outskirts or within the diagnosable reaches of the spectrum.

According to Harpur *et al.* (2003, pp.245–51), historical accounts and records suggest that the following notable individuals possessed various AS traits and characteristics:

- Nicola Tesla (1856–1943)—physicist
- Wolfgang Amadeus Mozart (1756–1791)—musician and composer
- Bela Bartòk (1881–1945)—musician and composer
- Erik Satie (1866–1925)—musician and composer
- Évariste Galois (1811–1832)—inventor of group theory
- Isaac Newton (1642–1727)—mathematician, scientist
- Albert Einstein (1879–1955)—mathematician, scientist
- Vincent van Gogh (1853–1890)—artist
- L.S. Lowry (1887–1976)—painter
- Andy Warhol (1928–1987)—pop art pioneer and avant-garde filmmaker
- Antonio Gaudi (1852–1926)—architect
- Jonathan Swift (1667–1745)—author, clergyman and propagandist
- Lewis Carroll (1832–1898)—author, clergyman, mathematician
- Hans Christian Andersen (1805–1875)—author
- Baruch Spinoza (1632–1677)—philosopher
- Immanuel Kant (1724–1804)—philosopher and theoretician
- Ludwig Wittgenstein (1889–1951)—philosopher
- Willard Van Orman Quine (1908–2000)—philosopher.

The authors further mention Thomas Jefferson and Eamon de Valera (politicians), Viscount Montgomery and Stonewall Jackson (military men), and Charles Lindbergh (aviator).

The following luminaries are among some of many who have received attention over the past few years as those who have accomplished remarkable feats in spite of being described by researchers, authors, clinicians, or at times themselves, as sharing a number of Asperger, or autism-like phenotypes. As described throughout various sources (some of which are noted here) these phenotypes have not only not impeded the attainment of their discoveries, attainments and fulfillment of their goals, but appear to have been factors, at times significantly, in the attainment of these accomplishments, many of which have contributed to the enhancement of our lives in various fields. It is important to mention that, whenever referring to the Asperger-like phenotypes that seem to be extant across these individuals, these have been consistently noted in a positive, self-affirming, and empowering light that has served to assist, rather than detract, from the realization of their endowments. Rather than presenting themselves as obstacles, deficits, or limitations, these phenotypes have been accessed by these remarkable individuals, and combined with training, education, personal motivation and ambition, and the support of caring individuals, to express themselves as *strengths* that have led to triumphs in their personal and professional lives.

Bram Cohen

BitTorrent is described as a preeminent, decentralized file distribution method which allows individuals or companies to share files without need for bandwidth demands. The creator of this remarkable program that has essentially helped to revolutionize the music world in particular, and the world of downloading and file-sharing over the Internet in general, Bram Cohen, diagnosed himself with Asperger's Syndrome at the age of 27. According to a *Time* article (Cohen 2005) "Bram Cohen was an unusual kid. While other first-graders were outside playing, he was writing computer code. By junior high, he could solve Rubik's Cube in a few minutes. A college dropout, he went on to co-found a hacker convention in San Francisco." Describing himself as "always really weird," he relates that diagnosing himself with AS helped to explain a number of his characteristics including social difficulties, obsession with puzzles, problems censoring his thoughts, and difficulties making eye contact.

Collin Merenoff

The co-founder of The Mechanical Advantage, a resource for the Pulley and Hay Camer Collector (www.themechanicaladvantage.com), Collin Merenoff is described as skilled in several programming languages, information technology, mathematics, fractal programming, and quantum theory. Aside from being described as sharing a number of several Asperger-like phenotypes by a number of sources, The Mechanical Advantage website indicates that Mr. Merenoff was diagnosed with high functioning autism, or Asperger's Syndrome, at the time of his birth. The website further indicates that his "life skills were nurtured while he worked on his special interests in mathematics and computer sciences" at a Special Education Program in Macomb County, Michigan.

Richard Borcherds: Nobel Prize in Mathematics
The Fields Medal is described as the equivalent of the Nobel Prize in mathematics and is reputed to be the highest accolade mathematicians can receive. The winner of the 1988 Fields Medal award, Richard Borcherds, received this great distinction for his work on "a topic so obscure that most mathematicians working in his former Cambridge University department are unable to understand what he is doing. His mathematical brilliance is unquestioned by other mathematicians, even if they cannot follow the specifics of his ideas" (Baron-Cohen 2003, p.155). Several writers have noted a number of Asperger-type qualities demonstrated by Professor Borcherds, qualities that have helped lead to some of his accomplishments in the fields of mathematics.

Paul Dirac: Lucasian Chair of Mathematics at Cambridge
The Lucasian Chair of Mathematics at Cambridge, the same professorship that has at times been held by Sir Isaac Newton and Stephen Hawking, was accorded to Paul Dirac (1902–1984). Between the ages of 23 and 31, he devised an interpretation of quantum mechanics which led to a quantum theory of the emission and absorption of radiation by atoms, the relativistic wave equation of the electron, the idea of anti-particles and even a theory of magnetic monopoles which distinguished him from his peers (Baron-Cohen 2003, p.166). The winner of the Nobel Prize at the remarkably young age of 31, Professor Dirac is another luminary who has been described as sharing a number of Asperger-like phenotypes.

Michael Ventris: Linear B

Michael Ventris (1922–1956) is perhaps best known as the man who cracked Linear B. According to world famous researcher and champion of the Asperger/autism cause, Dr. Simon Baron-Cohen of Cambridge University, Mr. Ventris was "the first person on the planet to be able to read and speak Linear B for 4000 years." According to Dr. Baron-Cohen, author himself of theories proposing a "systemizing" and mentalizing approach that helps to explain a number attributes of persons with Asperger's Syndrome, Mr. Ventris' motivation was "to crack the system—to systemize" (Baron-Cohen 2003, p.168).

Ludwig Wittgenstein: Philosopher

Wittgenstein has been described as "the most perfect example of an autistic philosopher." (Fitzgerald 2004, p.121). Placing him in the ranks of "Einstein, Freud, Turing, Yeats, Ramanujan and Russell as one of the intellectual giants of the twentieth century," Fitzgerald indicates that what Wittgenstein achieved was almost unattainable by most people's standards. Accounts that refer to Wittgenstein's characteristics as being similar to those with Asperger's Syndrome, or his "Asperger-phenotypes," are extant across the literature that describe his personal and professional approaches to the world.

Keith Joseph: "Founder of Modern Conservatism in Britain"

Described by Margaret Thatcher as "the founder of modern conservatism in Britain," Keith Joseph was renowned as one of the most influential British politicians of the late twentieth century (Fitzgerald 2004, p.143). "[He] shows the strengths and weaknesses of the politician with HFA/ASP. He was a sincere person but lacked the ability to empathize with individuals, groups and society. As a consequence, he tried to understand society using a mathematical approach, i.e., through statistics and economics" (Fitzgerald 2004, p.155).

Eamon de Valera: Politician and Mathematician

Another historical leading light who has been depicted as possessing a number of Asperger phenotype traits, Eamon de Valera, an Irish politician and mathematician, is described by Michael Fitzgerald as actually meeting the criteria for HFA/AS. He describes Mr. de Valera's contribution thus:

> Eamon de Valera is regarded as one of the great figures in Irish history…
> He played a central role in the foundation of the Irish State, moving from revolutionary to Prime Minister to President. In fact, several world leaders, and, indeed, a U.S. intelligence agent have attested to his political genius. A gifted mathematician also, he is reputed to have been one of nine people in the world capable of understanding Einstein's theory of relativity during the scientist's lifetime. (Fitzgerald 2004, p.157)

William Butler Yeats: Nobel Prize for Literature

The recipient of the Nobel Prize for Literature in 1923, the poet and playwright William Butler Yeats is well known as a genius in the field of literature as well as for his political contributions to the Irish state as senator during the 1920s. Having distinguished himself in many fields—as a poet, playwright, painter, theatre director, occultist, and political figure—the features he shared with those of Asperger's Syndrome seemed to contribute to many of his accomplishments (Fitzgerald 2004, p.170).

Lewis Carroll: Author

Universally renowned author Lewis Carroll's best-known, and perhaps most loved classic children's stories, *Alice's Adventures in Wonderland* and *Through the Looking Glass, and What Alice Found There*, ensured that the author, Lewis Carroll, became a household name in the hearts and minds of millions of readers of every age. According to Fitzgerald (2004), many accounts of Carroll's life indicate that "he clearly displayed significant features of HFA/ASP" (p.194).

Fitzgerald adds:

> Lewis Carroll shows that a person with HFA/ASP has a capacity for enormous imagination, even if of an immature kind. His HFA/ASP and his immature personality—part of the condition—attuned him to children and helped him to be one of the greatest writers of children's stories of all time. He had a mechanical-mathematical mind, which is highly characteristic of people with HFA/ASP. Other features of the condition that helped him be successful included his workaholism and extreme self-control. (Fitzgerald 2004, p.205)

Srinivasa Ramanujan: Mathematician

Considered by many to be India's greatest mathematician, Srinivasa Ramanujan, born in 1887, is often described as a genius who "independently changed the face of mathematics in the early twentieth century. His legacies in the field of analytical theory of numbers, elliptic functions, continued fractions and infinite series have reinvented modern mathematics…from an early age he showed clear signs of autism" (Fitzgerald 2004, p.206). Fitzgerald adds that "there is no doubt that Ramanujan met the criteria for HFA/ASP… The condition of HFA/ASP can be helpful for mathematicians because their work requires extraordinary levels of concentration, and if the person has little interest in human relationships this allows increased concentration and precludes distractions" (p.222).

Prominent Mathematicians, Scientists, and Creative Artists

Dr. Muhammad Arshad, a psychiatrist and researcher at Five Boroughs Partnership NHS Trust in Great Britain, and Professor Michael Fitzgerald of Trinity College in Dublin, Ireland, note in the *Journal of Medical Biography* (BBC News 1 June 2004) that Michelangelo had many of the traits associated with Asperger's Syndrome. Dr. Fitzgerald suggests in his book *In Autism and Creativity: Is There a Link Between Autism in Men and Exceptional Ability?* that a number of prominent mathematicians, scientists, and authors could be described as having AS based on "evidence drawn from autobiographical accounts or other people's contemporary descriptions of their behaviour." Among the historical figures Fitzgerald suggests as having shown signs of AS include Socrates, Charles Darwin, Andy Warhol, Isaac Newton, Albert Einstein, Lewis Carroll, W.B. Yeats, and former Irish prime minister Eamon de Valera. According to Professor Fitzgerald:

> Asperger's syndrome provides a plus—it makes people more creative. People with it are generally hyper-focused, very persistent workaholics who tend to see things from detail to global rather than looking at the bigger picture first and then working backwards, as most people do.

Regarding Michelangelo, Dr. Arshad draws his conclusions from a number of works, including notes from the artist's assistant and family (Arshad 2004, pp.115–120; BBC News 2003; BBC News 2004).

$\mathcal{A}$ ppendix: Data Collection Forms

Form A

Asperger related stories, quotes and other contributions

Do you have a favorite Asperger-related story, quote, or inspirational situation that you would like to share with us?

Dr. Ortiz is in the process of assembling a book to assist both laypersons and professionals to better understand children, teens and adults with Asperger's Syndrome and high functioning autism. Any special quote or situation that you feel would help to raise awareness to these fascinating conditions and which you would like to contribute would be well received. Stories and quotes can be inspirational, humorous, touching, or of any nature that you feel would assist others in better understanding persons with AS or HFA. Accounts can be as concise as a short comment, or a preferred topic or "passion," or as long as a few pages. If possible, please keep the lengthier submissions under 300 words.

Contributions will present the facts as submitted but preserve anonymity. Please send any contributions to:

> Dr. John M. Ortiz, Director and Founder
> The Asperger's Syndrome Institute
> P.O. Box 113
> Dillsburg, PA. 17109

Or email them to:

> DrO@asperger-institute.com

The story/quote I would like to contribute to Dr. Ortiz's book is:

_____

_____

_____

_____

_____

_____

_____

_____

_____

_____

_____

_____

_____

_____

_____

_____

_____

_____

If your contribution is selected may we have your permission to publish it?

Signed _____   Date_____

Form B

1) What is your (first) name?

(2) What is your age?

(3) What is your sex?

(4) What is your profession?

- Could you describe your work duties or responsibilities?

- Could you describe how you feel about your work or career?

- If in school: what grade are you in?

- If attending college or university: what is your major/field of specialty?

(5) Do you have any particular hobbies? If so, could you discuss them?

(6) Are you currently in a relationship?

(7) What would you say is your learning style (visual, auditory, verbal, physical, logical, social, solitary, or a combination of the above)?

(8) Is there anything else that you would like to share about yourself?

_____

_____

_____

_____

_____

_____

_____

_____

If your contribution is selected may we have your permission to publish it?

Signed _____   Date: _____

Recommended Books Written by Authors with Autism or Asperger's Syndrome

The Feeling's Mutual – Will Hadcroft

Congratulations! It's Asperger Syndrome – Jen Birch

Asperger Syndrome, the Universe and Everything – Kenneth Hall

Autism-Asperger and Sexuality – Jerry and Mary Newport

Your Life is not a Label – Jerry Newport and Ron Bass

Mozart and the Whale – Jerry Newport

Freaks, Geeks and Asperger Syndrome – Luke Jackson

Pretending to be Normal – Liane Holliday Willey

Beyond the Wall – Temple Grandin

Emergence Autistic – Temple Grandin

Thinking in Pictures – Temple Grandin

Aquamarine Blue 5 – Dawn Prince-Hughes

Asperger Syndrome and Long Term Relationships – Liane Holliday Willey

Asperger Syndrome in the Family – Liane Holliday Willey

A User Guide for the GF/CF Diet for Autism, AS and ADHD – Luke Jackson

Through the Eyes of Aliens – Jasmine Lee O'Neill

Demystifying the Autistic Experience – William Stillman

Understanding and Working with the Spectrum of Autism – Wendy Lawson

Build Your Own Life – Wendy Lawson

Finding Out About AS, High-Functioning Autism, and PDD – Gunila Gerland

Beyond the Wall – Stephen Shore

Asperger Syndrome Employment Workbook – Roger Meyer

Autism: An Inside-Out Approach – Donna Williams

Discovering my Autism – Edgar Schneider

Women From Another Planet – Jean Kearns Miller

Autism and Sensing – Donna Williams

Exposure Anxiety: The Invisible Cage – Donna Williams

Light on the Horizon – Thomas A. McKean

Sounds of Falling Snow – Annabel Stehli (editor)

On My Own Terms: My Journey With Asperger's – Robert Sanders Jr.

Overcoming Asperger's – Robert Sanders Jr.

Employment for Individuals with AS or NvLD – Yvona Fast

Recommended Internet Sites: Sites Worth Sighting and Citing

Unlocking Autism – www.unlockingautism.org. Accessed 6 November 2007.

Safe Minds – www.safeminds.org. Accessed 6 November 2007.

National Institute of Mental Health – www.nimh.nih.gov. Accessed 6 November 2007.

The Source (MAAP Services) – www.maapservices.org. Accessed 6 November 2007.

Autism Research Centre (ARC) – www.autismresearchcentre.com. Accessed 6 November 2007.

Autism and Asperger Research Reports – aarr.stanford.edu/banner.html. Accessed 6 November 2007.

Fighting Autism – www.fightingautism.org. Accessed 6 November 2007.

Green Chimneys – www.greenchimneys.org. Accessed 6 November 2007.

Cure Autism Now (CAN) – www.cureautismnow.org. Accessed 6 November 2007.

The Asperger's Syndrome Institute – www.asperger-institute.com. Accessed 6 November 2007.

Autinet Forum links page – www.iol.ie/~wise/autinet/anflinks.htm. Accessed 6 November 2007.

Jessica Kingsley Publishers – www.jkp.com. Accessed 6 November 2007.

Future Horizons – www.futurehorizons-autism.com. Accessed 6 November 2007.

Irlen Institute – www.irleninstitute.com. Accessed 6 November 2007.

Autism Independent UK – www.autismuk.com. Accessed 6 November 2007.

Asperger Syndrome Livejournal Community – www.livejournal.com/community/asperger. Accessed 6 November 2007.

Sideways Minds – www.tshirtrebel.com/sideways. Accessed 6 November 2007.

Families for Early Autism Treatment (FEAT) – www.feat.org. Accessed 6 November 2007.

Autism-info.com – www.autism-info.com. Accessed 6 November 2007.

Camp MakeBelieve – www.campmakebelievekids.com. Accessed 6 November 2007.

Sensory Resources – www.sensoryresources.com. Accessed 6 November 2007.

Autism Asperger Publishing Company – www.asperger.net. Accessed 6 November 2007.

OASIS – www.udel.edu/bkirby/asperger. Accessed 6 November 2007.

Tony Attwood – www.tonyattwood.com.au. Accessed 6 November 2007.

The National Autistic Society – www.nas.org.uk. Accessed 6 November 2007.

WrongPlanet.net – www.wrongplanet.net. Accessed 6 November 2007.

The Autism Picture Page – picturepage.net. Accessed 6 November 2007.

Autistic Adults Picture Project – www.isn.net/~jypsy/AuSpin/a2p22.html. Accessed 6 November 2007.

Delphi Forums – www.delphiforums.com. Accessed 6 November 2007.

Autism Research Institute (ARI) – www.autismwebsite.com. Accessed 6 November 2007.

The Asperger Marriage Web Site – www.asperger-marriage.info. Accessed 6 November 2007.

Aspergia: A new way of thinking – www.aspergia.com. Accessed 6 November 2007.

Asperger Syndrome Education Network (ASPEN) – www.aspennj.org. Accessed 6 November 2007.

Coping: A Survival Guide – www-users.cs.york.ac.uk/~alistair/survival. Accessed 6 November 2007.

Autism Arts – www.autismarts.com. Accessed 6 November 2007.

University Students with Autism and Asperger's – www.users.dircon.co.uk./ ~cns/index.html. Accessed 6 November 2007.

Oddizms – www.geocities.com/autistry/oddizms.html. Accessed 6 November 2007.

Aspergerinfo.com – www.aspergerinfo.com. Accessed 6 November 2007.

The Judevine Center for Autism – www.judevine.org. Accessed 6 November 2007.

References

Arshad, M. (2004) "What is autism?" *Journal of Medical Biography 12*, 115–20.

Asperger, H. (1991) "'Autistic Psychopathy' in Childhood" In U. Frith (ed.) *Autism and Asperger Syndrome*. New York, NY: Cambridge University Press.

Attwood, T. (1998) *Asperger's Syndrome: A Guide for Parents and Professionals*. Philadelphia, PA: Jessica Kingsley Publishers.

Baron-Cohen, S. (2003) *The Essential Difference: The Truth about the Male and Female Brain*. New York, NY: Basic Books.

Barrett, L. (2003) "Lessons from the Little Professor: Asperger's Syndrome: 'Wired Differently – Not Defectively.'" Available at: http://lisabarrettmann.com/Lessons_from_the_Little_Professor.html (accessed 7 January 2008).

BBC News (2003) "Brilliant Minds Linked to Autism." Available at: http://news.bbc.co.uk/1/hi/health/3380569.stm (accessed 7 January 2008).

BBC News (2004) "Michelangelo 'Linked' with Autism." Available at: http://news.bbc.co.uk/1/hi/entertainment/arts/3765509.stm (accessed 7 January 2008).

Bogdashina, O. (2003) *Sensory Perceptual Issues in Autism and Asperger Syndrome*. Philadelphia, PA: Jessica Kingsley Publishing.

Carroll, L. (1945) *Alice's Adventures in Wonderland and Through the Looking-Glass*. Originally published in 1865. Racine, WI: Whitman Publishing.

Cohen, B. (2005) *The BitTorrent Effect*. Available at www.wired.com/wired/archive/13.01/bittorrent.html. Accessed on 7 November 2007.

Connor, M. (2000) "Asperger syndrome (autistic spectrum disorder) and the self-reports of comprehensive school students." *Educational Psychology in Practice 16*, 3, 285–96.

Coursey, C. (2005) "Asperger's Syndrome Could Be a Character-builder." *ETC: A Review of General Semantics 62*, 308–309.

Davies, A. (2004) *Teaching Asperger's Students Social Skills through Acting: All their World's a Stage!* Arlington, TX: Future Horizons.

DSMIV-TR™ (2000) *Diagnostic Statistical Manual, Text Revision.* Washington, DC: American Psychiatric Association.

Fast, Y. (2004) *Employment for Individuals with Asperger Syndrome or Non-verbal Learning Disability.* Philadelphia, PA: Jessica Kingsley Publishers.

Fitzgerald, M. (2004) *Autism and Creativity: Is there a Link between Autism in Men and Exceptional Ability?* New York, NY: Brunner-Routledge.

Gillberg, C. (2002) *A Guide to Asperger's Syndrome.* New York, NY: Cambridge University Press.

Grandin, T. (1995) *Thinking in Pictures: And Other Reports from My Life with Autism.* New York, NY: Vintage Books.

Grandin, T. and Duffy, K. (2004) *Developing Talents: Careers for Individuals with Asperger Syndrome and High-Functioning Autism.* Shawnee Mission, KS: Autism Asperger Publishing Co.

Haddon, Mark (2002) *The Curious Incident of the Dog in the Night-Time.* New York, NY: Doubleday.

Hall, K. (2001) *Asperger Syndrome, the Universe and Everything.* Philadelphia, PA: Jessica Kingsley Publishers.

Harpur, J. Lawlor, M. and Fitzgerald, M. (2003) *Succeeding in College with Asperger Syndrome.* Philadelphia, PA Jessica Kingsley Publishers.

Henderson, L.M. (2000) "Asperger's syndrome in gifted individuals." *Gifted Child Today 24*, 3, 28–35.

Hermelin, B. (2001) *Bright Splinters of the Mind: A Personal Story of Research with Autistic Savants.* Philadelphia, PA: Jessica Kingsley Publishers.

Huebner, R.A. (2001) *Autism: A Sensorimotor Approach to Management.* Austin, TX: PRO-ED, Inc.

Jackson, L. (2002) *Freaks, Geeks and Asperger Syndrome: A User Guide to Adolescence.* Philadelphia, PA: Jessica Kingsley Publishers.

Jacobs, B. (2003) *Loving Mr. Spock: Understanding an Aloof Lover.* Arlington, TX: Future Horizons.

Kennedy, D.M. (2002) *The ADHD-Autism Connection: A Step Toward More Accurate Diagnosis and Effective Treatment.* Colorado Springs, CO: WaterBrook Press.

Klin, A., Volkmar, F.R. and Sparrow, S.S. (eds) (2000) *Asperger Syndrome.* New York, NY: The Guilford Press.

Lawson, W. (2003) *Build Your Own Life: A Self-Help Guide for Individuals with Asperger's Syndrome.* Philadelphia, PA: Jessica Kingsley Publishers.

Ledgin, N. (2002) *Asperger's and Self-Esteem: Insight and Hope through Famous Role Models.* Arlington, TX: Future Horizons.

Lovecky, D.V. (2004) *Different Minds: Gifted Children with AD/HD, Asperger Syndrome, and Other Learning Disabilities.* Philadelphia, PA: Jessica Kingsley Publishers.

Mawhood, L. and Howlin, P. (1999) "The outcome of a supported employment scheme for high-functioning adults with autism or Asperger syndrome." *Autism 3*, 229–54.

Miller, J.K. (2003) *Women from Another Planet: Our Lives in the Universe of Autism.* Bloomington, IN: Dancing Mind Books.

Molloy, H. and Vasil, L. (2002) "The social construction of Asperger syndrome: The pathologising of difference?" *Disability and Society 17*, 659–69.

Moore, S.T. (2002) *Asperger Syndrome and the Elementary School Experience: Practical Solutions for Academic and Social Difficulties.* Shawnee Mission, KS: Autism Asperger Publishing Co.

Myles, B.S., Cook, K.T., Miller, N.E., Rinner, L. and Robbins, L.A. (2002) *Asperger Syndrome and Sensory Issues: Practical Solutions for Making Sense of the World.* Shawnee Mission, KS: Autism Asperger Publishing Co.

Myles, B.S. and Southwick, J. (1999) *Asperger Syndrome and Difficult Moments: Practical Solutions for Tantrums, Rage, and Meltdowns.* Shawnee Mission, KS: Autism Asperger Publishing Co.

Osbourne, L. (2000) "The little professor syndrome." *New York Times Magazine,* June 18, pp.6–12.

Ozonoff, S., Dawson, G. and McPartland, J. (2002) *A Parent's Guide to Asperger Syndrome and High-Functioning Autism: How to Meet the Challenges and Help your Child Thrive.* New York, NY: The Guilford Press.

Ponnet, K.S., Roeyers, H., Buysse, A., De Clercq, A. and Van Der Heyden, E. (2004) "Advanced mind-reading in adults with Asperger syndrome." *Autism 8*, 3, 249–66.

Prince-Hughes, D. (2002) *Aquamarine Blue Five: Personal Stories of College Students with Autism.* Athens, OH: Swallow Press.

Sacks, O. (1995) *An Anthropologist on Mars.* New York, NY: Vintage Books.

Shore, S. (2003) *Beyond the Wall: Personal Experiences with Autism and Asperger Syndrome.* 2nd edition. Shawnee Mission, KS: Autism-Asperger Publishing Co.

Sicile-Kira, C. (2004) *Autism Spectrum Disorders: The Complete Guide to Understanding Autism, Asperger's Syndrome, Pervasive Developmental Disorder, and other ASDs.* New York, NY: Perigee.

Stoddart, K.P. (2005) *Children, Youth and Adults with Asperger Syndrome: Integrating Multiple Perspectives.* Philadelphia, PA: Jessica Kingsley Publishers.

Szatmari, P. (2004) *A Mind Apart: Understanding Children with Autism and Asperger Syndrome.* New York, NY: Guilford Press.

Van Tassel-Baska, J. (1998) *Excellence in Educating Gifted and Talented Learners.* 3rd edition. Denver, CO: Love.

Willey, L.H. (2001) *Asperger Syndrome in the Family.* Philadelphia, PA: Jessica Kingsley Publishers.

Willey, L.H. (ed.) (2003) *Asperger Syndrome in Adolescence: Living with the Ups, the Downs and Things in Between.* Philadelphia, PA: Jessica Kingsley Publishers.

Williams, D. (1992) *Nobody Nowhere: The Extraordinary Autobiography of an Autistic.* New York, NY: Times Books.